Creating a Beautiful Landscape

Henry Rehder's Daily Guide

Creating a Beautiful Landscape
Henry Rehder's Daily Guide

By Henry Rehder, Jr.

First Edition

Coastal Carolina Press
Wilmington, NC

Creating a Beautiful Landscape: Henry Rehder's Daily Guide
Henry Rehder

Published by
Coastal Carolina Press
4709 College Acres Drive, Suite 1
Wilmington, North Carolina 28403 U.S.A.
www.coastalcarolinapress.org

First Edition

Edited by Emily Colin and Page Lowry
Book designed by Jane Baldridge/Artspeaks
Photographs by Michael Wolf, Freda Wilkins, Rob Gardner/NC Botanical Gardens
Cover: garden of Henry Rehder, Sr., Wilmington, NC, photo by Freda Wilkins

Printed in Canada

Applied for Library of Congress Cataloging-in-Publication Data

ISBN 1-928556-10-8

This book is dedicated to my mother and father, Barbara Beeland Rehder and Henry Burbank Rehder, who raised me in their gardens and libraries, showed me the beauty of God's creations, and taught me the Good News of The Gospel of Jesus.

IN MEMORIAM
Johanna Howerton Rehder
1977-1995

Freda Wilkins

ACKNOWLEDGEMENTS

I owe a special thanks to many gardeners and landscapers, both professional and amateur, who have spent much time sharing their knowledge of lawns and gardens with others. They taught me or refined every method I have of growing plants and flowers in the coastal gardens of the South. In many ways, this book is a tribute to them.

The late Reid Lassiter gave me the opportunity to tend his garden. Reid was a naturalist who employed many experimental and creative gardening techniques. Some of his practices were well ahead of his time, some old-fashioned. Reid was unselfish with his time and property.

I appreciate the advice and friendship of David Vann Barkley, urban horticulturist at the New Hanover County Extension Service Arboretum. Dr. C. Bruce Williams and John Cain are good friends who are always willing to share.

Thanks to the Master Gardeners Association of New Hanover County, the folks who operate the Master Gardeners' Hotline and plant clinics, for their support.

I extend a special thanks to my prayer partner and landscaper, Kenny Kwiatek, and to Aimee Schooley, a horticulturist of the first order.

Page Lowry is a patient editor and a gardening inspiration who challenges the obvious and always encourages excellence in garden culture.

Thanks to the editors and staff at Coastal Carolina Press, especially Emily Colin and Chris Compton, for their support and professional courtesies, advice and valuable assistance. They are much more than publishers. Jane Baldridge, as always, brings so much creativity to any work.

To Les and Ann Turlington of Farmers Supply Company, I offer profound thanks. I appreciate the sponsorship of Cross Garden Center: Tom, Janet and Jimmy.

For over ten years the media has supported the "Dr. Plant" series with an open door for horticulture and garden formats. I am in debt to Carl Venters of Ocean Broadcasting, Jon Evans and Kim Kopka of WWAY-TV 3, videographer Mark Simpson and Joe and Peggy Stanley of *Scene Magazine*. I thank my broadcast partner and engineer Pat Shipman, media representative Jack Britton, and Bill "JJ" Jefferay for many years of friendship.

Donn Ansell of WAAV's *Talk of The Town* began the "Dr. Plant" series in 1988, and Bob Townsend of WECT-TV 6's *Carolina in The Morning* has provided me with many opportunities to inform the public about caring for their lawns and gardens.

Thanks to Eric Higgins for coining the phrase "Dr. Plant," to John Misenheimer for leading me through troubled waters, to Ann Willard for opening her garden to me, to the staff and management of Oakdale Cemetery for allowing me time in their gardens, and to Kenneth Sprunt Sr. and Kenneth Sprunt, Jr. of Orton Plantation, home of the coastal South's most beautiful display of camellias and azaleas.

Editor and prayer partner Mark Opgrand is a faithful and patient friend.

My associate and business partner, Laura Jean Houghton, has been my favorite source of gardening advice. Without her help, writing this book would not have been possible.

Thanks to my family, especially Stanley Rehder, for his assistance and encouragement over the years. Stan taught me how to grow at his cooperative farm, and all of my knowledge on insectivorous plants has come from him.

I am indebted to my friend William W. "Bill" Muench.

I appreciate the friendship of William H. "Bill" MacKay.

My wife, Diane, and my daughter, Barbara Gaines, have been my biggest supporters throughout this project. Through hurricanes, computer crashes, family crises, and moments of great joy, they have been constant companions. Diane has been this book's guardian. I am humbled and honored by their support.

I thank my God, The Creator of the Universe, His Holy Spirit and my Savior, Jesus Christ.

Michael Wolf

TABLE OF CONTENTS

Freda Wilkins

INTRODUCTION

GARDENING IN THE COASTAL PLAIN

The greatest joy in coastal gardening is the success you can enjoy from your first efforts, even if you are a novice gardener. The reasons for this success include the climate we enjoy, the remarkable weather we experience and the soils in which we raise our flowers, ornamental shrubs, and trees.

CLIMATE

Here in the coastal Southeast, the growing season is long, and the prevailing temper of the environment is mild. Rainfall is adequate, and though we have wind in some months, we are not bothered by long periods of windy weather. A region's climate is defined by how these three meteorological conditions—temperature, rainfall, and wind—prevail over a long period of time. The Southeast coast is fortunate to have an excellent climate for gardening. Typically, spring comes early; summer is the longest of the seasons; fall lasts well into December; and winter is over by the last week in February. In this part of the country, the seasons fade into each other rather than abruptly changing. A chilly fall night might be followed by several days of summer-like warmth, and the cold, blustery days of autumn, so common just fifty miles west of the coast, are rare. Daffodils frequently bloom in January. Forsythia is apt to flower in December. Azaleas often show color in November, and the summer heat can temporarily halt even abelia from blossoming in August and September.

Clearly, the choices we make in landscape plants reflect that climate. We tend to select plants that survive well in our warm winters. Gardenias, crepe myrtles, and camellias are grown successfully here, while plants that need deeper chilling—peonies and lilacs, for example—simply will not thrive in coastal Carolina.

Newcomers to this area often view the climate in relation to the garden as confusing and unpredictable, since some flowers appear to bloom out of season. However, the climate of the coastal area has remained steady over time, and such plants probably act that way every year. Sunlight, soil temperature, atmospheric temperature, moisture, and plant nutrition all play a role in flower-making. When these conditions are right, a plant will bloom. In the coastal South, that frequently happens when least expected. Summer heat can cause dormancy in some plants, just as a January thaw can create flowering in others.

Overall, the climate of the coast creates a remarkable growing environment—one which offers a few challenges but also many rewards. If we accept our climate as a blessing, then we can appreciate some of the gardening surprises more easily. Tulips, planted in November to bloom in April, may sprout a few months early. An early summer heat wave may stop hydrangeas from flowering in late June. Over the course of years, these events have become quite normal and simply illustrate the nature of our climate. As you read the garden calendar and the scheduled tasks and chores, remember that our climate offers many opportunities, including changing the gardening schedules to suit climatic events.

WEATHER

The climate of a region is a picture of average weather conditions over a long period of time, and weather is a description of the meteorological events that take place during that period. We have a great variety of weather events here along the coast! A freak storm in the late 1980s dropped twelve inches of snow in a small area of the coast, while inland, the winter sun shone bright and clear. One blustery March day in 1990, the coastal plain experienced near hurricane-force winds, driving salty ocean spray several miles inland. Of course, our region has been a magnet for massive hurricanes, many of which, in recent years, have severely damaged the area. Summer storms flood the coast; freezing weather often frosts the region; and there can be times in any season when much-needed rain pours just out of range to the north or south.

Weather conditions along the coast are complicated and often unpredictable. Because we are so close to the Atlantic Ocean and the Gulf Stream, we are subject to rapidly changing patterns.

Some types of landscape plants are at home in these fickle weather patterns, and are so comfortable in the region they have become durable, solid sentinels in coastal gardens. They are usually of two types: **native plants** and **adapted plants**. **Native plants**, which were here when the first Europeans arrived, include wax myrtles, Yaupon, and American holly. **Adapted plants** are hybrids which were bred in other parts of the world and imported to the region by settlers. Gardenias, crepe myrtles, and most azaleas are just a few examples. In either case, native or adapted, these ornamental shrubs have remarkable lasting ability to not only "enjoy" the climate, but also survive quickly changing-weather conditions. Carolina bay, a native variety of magnolia, thrives in our warm, humid climate, but will also tolerate brief periods of severe freezing weather. The magnificent Burford holly, an adapted species of plant that is ideal for the coastal environment, does well in cold weather and tolerates salt spray. Native plants and most adapted ornamentals have become staples in the coastal landscape, not only because they like the long growing season, but also because they adjust quickly to periods of drought and high heat.

But quickly-changing weather patterns can cause unexpected problems for nearly any plant in the garden. For example, almost every winter brings a rapid deep freeze that desiccates the foliage of oleanders, resulting in the need to drastically prune freeze-damaged stems and branches. If a freeze takes place late in the winter, this severe pruning can slow the blooming cycle later in the summer. Long dry periods in the summer can kill perennial garden favorites such as daylilies and can cause enough stress in azaleas to kill entire branches. Both native and adapted plants usually survive these ups and downs, but there are some plants that simply won't make it when exposed to our weather conditions.

People who move to the coastal South from other areas of the country may find that the plants they bring with them cannot survive such unusual and varied growing conditions. If you have brought a favorite landscape plant from another part of the country, be prepared for it to struggle to adapt. I should also mention that some hybrid plants that have become popular in coastal gardens might eventually prove to be unsuited for the area because they have not stood the test of time. Bradford pears, though popular, may not be able to tolerate high winds, salt spray, and bark-splitting quick freezes.

The garden calendar section does not consider adverse weather conditions even though they are bound to happen. Offshore storms are frequent, for example, but their occurrences are unpredictable. Certain tasks may have to be postponed for a day or so, or may have to be advanced when these situations occur. The "how-to" section discusses storm damage, freeze damage and floodwater control, because storms, freezes, and floods are an integral part of coastal living.

COASTAL SOILS: SAND AND SWAMP

Alluvial soils were deposited by geological events in years past and have not been modified. There are several types found in the Southern coastal plain. Many horticulturists assume that most homeowners and gardeners in the coastal plain have sandy soil, because sand is the most frequently encountered soil base. In recent years, however, neighborhoods and entire suburban communities have been built on drained wetlands and in flood zones that, before being cleared and developed, were home to scrub pines and wilderness-type brambles and dense undergrowth. The soil in these areas is dense, poorly drained, and frequently wet.

Sandy soil is alluvial, and has some distinct characteristics: it drains rapidly, retains little nutrition and can often be so acidic in nature it may require yearly lime applications. Developed "bottom land" is also alluvial, and has the exact opposite consistency; it is often "sour" in nature, drains poorly, usually stays wet, and is even more acidic than sand.

Neither of these soil types is ideally suited for growing a beautiful garden, so changing the nature of the soil, or modifying it, is essential. Modifying the soil can require different methods. If the soil is sandy, and you want to increase its "bulk," the standard procedure is to condition it with compost or additional humus. This task can be done almost any time during the year. By contrast, heavy, wet soils are best modified during the dry periods of early summer and fall, when this type of garden soil can be easily worked. This task requires adding sand or some other porous material to lighten the texture and consistency of the soil. The job can be so intensive, however, that creating raised beds for garden plants may be preferable to growing a garden in wet soil or tackling a major renovation of the site.

If you want to grow a healthy garden, you will probably have to modify the soil consistency, whether it is light and sandy or dark and wet. Also, native soils have changed in recent years and have lost large amounts of major plant nutrients, trace elements, and micronutrients. The increased development of homesites that has been responsible for the extraction of these elements has also added storm water run-off, excessive synthetic fertilizers, and pollution to lawns and gardens. For successful gardening, these conditions will have to be altered.

If you decide to modify your garden soil, the garden calendar specifies a date to do so, but before bringing in a load of topsoil or renting a garden tiller, make sure you understand your soil type. This knowledge is a requirement before attempting to change its make-up.

Experts recommend that a complete soil test be done at least once every two years. The calendar will suggest a good time for this—usually in the fall of the year. Flag this date as one of the more important gardening dates, as soil testing is crucial to successful gardening. When you have received the results of the soil test, take steps to develop the best soil possible for your garden. Jane Farley, a noted perennial expert and horticulturist, advises her clients to budget first for soil conditioning and then for actual stock. She knows that the soil base is crucial to excellent plant performance, and that a good garden soil can make the difference between a landscape that thrives and one that merely exists.

Most gardeners agree that humus-rich soil is the best soil in which to grow plants. Until several years ago, humus generally had equal amounts of sand, clay, and organic matter, the result being a friable blend that promoted premium plant growth. But recently, horticulturists have placed an increased importance on the organic material in humus.

Organic matter contains natural nutrients, soil conditioners and microbes that enhance plant performance. Organic matter also serves to neutralize the pH of garden soil. The most reliable source of organic matter is compost, which is available commercially. The garden calendar stresses the importance of using compost as a soil conditioner both in the garden and on the lawn.

GROWING THE "SOUTHERN CLASSICS"

Some plants in the landscape thrive in just about any condition; they require little attention, are pest-free, and do quite well without interference. Typically, they do not tolerate being moved, but once established, they grace the garden with years of profound beauty. These are the classic landscape plants of the coastal South, the ones that have made Southern horticulture famous.

Many of these naturally thriving plants have been here for thousands of years, and were here long before the region was "discovered." These are the plants that have become so popular in maintenance-free landscapes, natural gardens and informal settings. Because they survive changing weather conditions and thrive in the general climate, native plants account for a large percentage of nursery stock sold to homeowners.

Modern homeowners have many demands on their time and many recreational opportunities other than maintenance of the lawn and garden. When time for landscaping is limited, native plants become ideal choices. They require little pruning and grooming, seldom need fertilizers, tolerate a wide range of soil conditions and sunlight exposures, and survive periods of both drought and heavy rains.

Native plants need not be restricted to wild or natural areas and can easily be fitted into more structured landscapes. In fact, the more natives you include in your garden, the less time you'll spend tending the overall landscape. You'll find that you spend much more time with adapted plants, and that caring for native plants will be a minor part of lawn and garden care. The garden calendar section offers guidelines for their care and maintenance.

There are quite a few from which to choose; you'll enjoy wax myrtles and Carolina cherry laurels as excellent hedges and screening plants. Yaupon attracts Spanish moss, has bumper crops of red berries, and is pest-free. Button bush is ideal for wetlands, creek banks and side-of-the-pond plantings, and American holly makes a striking tree with brightly-colored bark, dark green foliage and red berries for the holidays. Bay trees, Gordonia, and Eastern redbuds make superb tall shrubs and trees, Dahoon holly is an excellent border for the natural area, and loblolly and longleaf pines can be planted to replace those lost in storms.

But if native plants have so many positive attributes, adapted species of plants deserve an equal place in the coastal garden. When adapted plants were brought to the area many years ago by settlers and gardeners, these sturdy and durable selections greatly expanded the local choices. Gardenias, camellias, azaleas, and such classics as spirea and abelia are all adapted plants. Usually oriental in origin, these plants not only add great appeal to the coastal region, but in some cases have made the region famous. Azaleas are oriental plants that came to this area via England and Belgium. Because they originated in areas that have growing conditions similar to those of the coastal South, they were right at home in the soils of the area, and quickly became popular as carefree plants that could tolerate a number of conditions, while producing beautiful flowers and foliage.

Because adapted plants form the nucleus of the ornamental flower garden, and because homeowners require them to perform at peak levels, they are the plants that are emphasized in the garden section. Dates for pruning, feeding and transplanting are crucial for these plants, as are methods of pest control. The recommended dates for maintaining good garden sanitation are also important. With azaleas, for example, cleaning the old mulch away from the plants is an important late-winter chore, just as pruning forsythia in March is crucial to next year's blooming.

Most modern gardens contain several hybrid plants, some of which have become quite popular in the coastal South. These hybrids may be strong plants which have a great deal of appeal to the region's gardens, such as Leyland cypress and the dwarfed varieties of old standards like magnolia and Burford holly. But hybrids can also be susceptible to many pests and diseases, and in some cases are simply poor selections for the coastal garden. Some boxwoods fall into this group, as do several varieties of azaleas. Other hybrids, those with unusual growth habits or brightly colored foliage, (e.g. Nandina 'Firepower' or golden euonymous) may be popular for the moment, but may never acquire classic status. Such plants often sacrifice strength and vigor for color and variegation. Sickly and prone to infection, they do not succeed as great plants. The garden calendar section and the "how-to" section cover these plants in a cursory fashion.

"Revival" plants, however, are covered extensively, and the calendar section mentions many of them in detail. Revival plants are those which have recently become more popular in coastal landscapes after spending some time on the back shelf. Once quite common in the South, they may have fallen into disfavor because of cultivation problems, or because they did not fit into the sophisticated garden schemes of the 1960s and '70s.

Ginger lilies were once the pride of the rural Southern garden, but because they require so much space, and do not fit well into structured settings, they were all but forgotten for several decades. Now these lilies, along with several other old-world garden staples, are showing significant signs of popularity as homeowners are more willing to allow the space and time necessary to cultivate such plants. *Weigela florida* is a good example; though it requires a large space in which to grow and some annual pruning, many gardeners find the wonderful spring blooms worth the effort. The same is true for abelia and spirea, both of which fell from favor in recent years, but have now become more popular. Because of the increased interest in these plants, and the fact that many of them are classic Old South plants, they are mentioned by name. There are specific dates and tasks for caring for these wonderful revived selections.

Of course, knowing what plants will grow well in the coastal South may lead you to choose those plants for your garden and it will certainly eliminate some choices. If you are unsure about a specific selection, and you don't find it mentioned in the book, take a look around the neighborhood and see if you find it in another garden. If not, chances are good that it will not perform well here, even if you find it for sale at one of the larger home and garden centers. This book deals with landscape plants from a positive view; if they will grow in the coastal South, the calendar, with its dates and tips, will help you cultivate them to their best possible appearance. Marginally successful plants that have to be treated constantly for mere survival are not included.

In choosing plants for your landscape, you may have to leave some old favorites behind. Cool season-turf, such as fescue, can't stand the heat for very long. MacIntosh apples are great for cooler areas of the country, but won't make a decent crop here. Lilacs and peonies are Northern staples, but never perform well in the warm gardens of the coast.

Certainly, very good substitutes for your old favorites can be found. In fact, you may be so pleased with the "second choice" that you'll forget about the lost plants as you develop an appreciation for something new. And when you do, this daily garden companion will suit your purposes just fine!

SOME OTHER CONSIDERATIONS

Local gardening traditions are important in any part of the country and they influence the way people raise their flowers and landscape plants. This is particularly true along the coast of the South because the region is only a few generations removed from an agrarian society. Since the coastal regions were settled before most other areas inland, people who tend the gardens and landscapes of the area take pride in the way they are cultivated.

This area is home to some wonderful old gardens. Orton Plantation and Airlie Gardens are sites with great history and remarkable displays of flowers, trees, and ornamental shrubbery in many settings, both formal and natural. Not all gardens have to follow those examples; there are many beautiful landscapes that do not contain the plants for which the region is famous. Azaleas, for example, though popular in many landscape schemes because they symbolize traditional coastal garden beauty, may not fit well into some modern garden designs. Large live oaks are picturesque and reminiscent of old South charm, but they are rare in most home gardens. Many gardeners live in patio homes, condominiums, and complexes with shared open spaces that are not landscaped in traditional style. Though you may want to try some of the plants that have made many regional gardens famous, don't feel obligated by the great traditions of coastal gardens.

You will find frequent references to small shade trees. The shade from the canopy of such trees, and the resulting dappled sunlight which falls on the garden, is essential for good plant performance. Even though many coastal plants are rated for "full sun," you'll find that most plants perform best when direct sunlight is slightly shaded. Small flowering shrubs such as gardenias and camellias are perfect examples.

Keeping some plants cool and shaded is only one reason for growing a few shade trees; we have lost many small shade trees to recent storms and should replace them. Furthermore, these trees complement other plants in the landscape. They accent the colors of plants beneath them, form excellent backgrounds for shrubs, are often the first things to bloom in the spring, and add brilliant color to the autumn sky.

You can certainly grow many of the landscape plants mentioned in the book, but small shade trees may be even more enjoyable as they will bring years of pleasure to your gardening. You'll find them attractive for birdhouses and feeders, wind chimes, and even swings. Most of all, they'll add vitality to your landscape. The calendar includes many recommendations that will enhance the vigor of these landscape guardians.

Included are several references to lawn grass; in fact, nearly every calendar month has a day or so marked for turf management. In today's landscape, lawns assume a prominent place. While it is regrettable that they are often the criteria by which we judge the overall beauty of a garden, a premium appearance begins with the grass. Cultivating healthy turf is not easy in the coastal South and our lawns face many problems, from simple cultivation flukes to major diseases. An excess or a deficit of water can create huge problems, and lawn pests can quickly kill whole sections of the yard. Warm-season turf is naturally tough and resilient and, when healthy, you'll find it thick in texture, rich in color, and soft on your feet. Maintaining a healthy weed-free lawn requires some diligent effort, but if you follow the calendar closely, tend your lawn a little all year rather than just during the growing season, and solve problems quickly, you'll have a lawn that will be the pride of the neighborhood.

There are some distinct advantages to living along the coast, advantages that include hobbies other than tending the lawn and garden. The growing season, which is also the season for so many other pastimes, should not be taken up totally with mowing the lawn and pruning the hedges. The garden calendar is flexible, and some of the tasks and chores can be shuffled or even put off until a later date. But if you do a little all along, you'll have more spare time for grilling, golfing, and boating. For instance, I enjoy outdoor sports, fishing and hunting, so I have tried to spread a lot of chores over the year.

The garden calendar is a direct result of requests from folks who want to simplify their lawn and garden activities, and the garden "how to" guide is a natural accompaniment to this calendar. As you go through the garden calendar, I hope you'll discover new techniques, new ideas, and maybe some new times of the year to enjoy favorite garden activities. There is room on the pages for you to make your own notes. After a year with your garden calendar companion, I hope you'll look back on it as you would a journal, and that the tips included will have helped to make your year easier, more organized, and especially, lots of fun. I wish you all the best and many great gardening years!

HOW TO USE THIS BOOK

THE CALENDAR

Although garden maintenance is a year-round job, the large tasks can be spread over a broad period, which makes for an easier, more pleasant workload. To be sure, there are times when you'll have some heavy lifting. But, for the most part, life is simpler if the chores are spread over a long period of time. For example, installing a weed-blocking fabric mulch over the daylily bed can be done when the daylilies first break dormancy, but there might be other tasks in the spring garden that will require your attention at the same time. Therefore, this book will recommend that you tackle the chore in January, long before the daylilies show up, and when the days are not so crowded with tasks. Improvements we make in the garden during one season may have a direct effect on the garden during another. Liming the annual color garden to improve soil pH should be done six months before annuals bloom, because it takes that long for limestone to change soil from acid to alkaline. Changing the color of hydrangeas from blue to pink also takes a while; that's why the calendar addresses the soil around hydrangeas in October and November. There is something to do, some chore or task, in the lawn and garden nearly every day of the year. Some of those tasks, like changing the pH of the soil, relate to future performance.

From the very first day of January (the beginning of the winter season), through the entire year, you'll find suggestions for maintaining your landscape. You can use the calendar much as you would a garden journal, following the recommended schedules and chores and making notes as you need them. The calendar is divided into "seasons" which coincide roughly with the traditional garden seasons. Each calendar section provides an overview of the landscape in that season, an outline of its appearances, typical weather conditions, some practices to avoid, and some activities to perform.

Some dates are fixed and specific for certain tasks because they do not depend on weather conditions. For example, February 15th is marked as a date to bring tropical hibiscus plants out of storage, for example, because regardless of the weather that day, it will be time to fertilize them and expose them to more direct light. June 20th is designated as a day for pruning poinsettia plants, a job that can be done in just about any weather situation.

Other jobs will have to be adjusted in the calendar because of weather. March 10th may not be an ideal day to remove the mulch from beneath azalea beds. Labor Day may not be suitable for fertilizing the lawn. Moving tasks around the calendar is certainly going to happen, and is perfectly acceptable, so long as the general timetable is kept.

THE "HOW TO" SECTION

The calendar will give a date for a specific job, but you might be unsure of just how to do it. The last week in February is an ideal time to apply a lawn grass herbicide with a hose-end sprayer, but you may not be sure how to use the tool. In fact, hose-end sprayers are not simple to load and dispense, and many homeowners have trouble using them. The "how to" section of the book takes some of the mystery out of ordinary garden chores, including using specialized equipment, pruning some plants, and deciding which pesticide to use.

The garden calendar is not exact because nature is not exact. However, it is important to be precise when using tools, following safety measures, and mixing chemicals. There is some room for play in the calendar, but not much in the "how to" section.

Throughout the book you will find marginal notes which include simple recipes, tips, anecdotes, and ideas from many sources. Often they will save some time and energy. In some cases they will explain little-known facts about specific plants that will help solve a problem or get jobs done a little more easily. Sometimes they relate to the subject on the page, sometimes not.

Freda Wilkins

THE SPRING GARDEN:
MARCH, APRIL, AND MAY

No garden season is more exciting than spring, if for no other reason than dormancy is broken and nearly everything in the landscape comes alive. Though there have been a few warm, balmy days in winter, by the second week in March, cold days and nights are usually over, and moderate temperatures prevail. Spring usually comes easily to the region, arriving in obvious fashion, with all the color and vibrancy for which it is famous. Some of the late-winter blooming plants, camellias and daphne, for example, still show color, and will continue to do so for a few more weeks. Those that gave an early hint of their bloom potential, such as forsythia and quince, suddenly burst into full flower. Flowering fruit trees, including Bradford pears and ornamental peaches, quickly make abundant blossoms, and the spectacular display from bulbs, such as tulips and jonquils, blooms in nearly every landscape. Winter may leave with a last-minute gust, but by the middle of March, lawns and gardens are pushing the damp, cold conditions out of the way, and the landscape literally comes alive.

And it does so in all areas of the garden, from the lawn grass to the tallest shade tree. Soil and atmospheric temperatures rise as sunlight becomes more intense and longer in duration. Plants are "signaled" to begin growth, and though this takes place at various times depending on the species, dormancy—the hibernation of plant life—is broken. In a good year, when spring comes quickly, an abundance of plants, flowers, and trees can be in simultaneous bloom. In other years, color in the landscape may come more gradually.

The first of the large trees to flower are usually the maples with their orange-red flowers and winged fruits, followed by the greening of bald cypress and the small flowers of tupelos, cottonwoods and sweet gums. A few weeks later, poplars and river birches begin to foliate. Smaller shade trees, particularly flowering ones, offer the first major display of spring color. Most notable are the hybrid magnolias with their pink and white saucer-shaped flowers. Chinese hollies, which are some of the first small trees to flower, are often susceptible to late cold snaps. Their ability to produce plenty of red holly berries seven months later depends on a warm, fast spring; a late spring freeze can eliminate the presence of red berries for the holidays. Plums, pears, and some of the other trees that produce fruit are also susceptible to the damaging effects of late freezes.

If the timing is right for mid-March flowering, the show can be spectacular. Magenta-colored redbuds blooming above canopies of white dogwoods can be breathtaking, while Oriental cherry trees and American plums make stunning displays. Later, in late March or early April, crabapples put on their exquisite show.

Spring gardens may be most famous for their bulbs. Snowdrops, daffodils, tulips, and

Freda Wilkins

hyacinths all flower in the early days of spring. Although late-winter blooming is not uncommon, most bulbs will bloom on schedule when the soil is warm. One of the surprises of the spring garden is discovering jonquils and crocuses that were planted back in the late fall. Forgotten for several months, they emerge to the delight of unsuspecting gardeners.

The classic beauty of the great ornamentals truly typifies the coastal spring garden. Azaleas and spireas, weigelas and deutzia, sweet mock orange, and viburnums all bloom in the early days of April, and the flowers often last well into the first few days of May. Horticulturists often refer to these plants as "classics" because they have endured in the Southern coastal landscape, thriving in all sorts of conditions. In many cases, these are the species that were brought here by the first European settlers, and they have adapted to the local climate and the soil conditions. Though modern trends in gardening have encouraged the planting of newer hybrids, exceptional plants, and ornamentals with variegated foliage and unusual blooming habits, the classic "look" and "feel" of the stately old guardians brings spring to the coastal landscape. It's no wonder that gardeners across the region purchase and plant more classic ornamentals in the spring than any other time of the year. It's during March, April, and May that we see them at their best, and it's in the spring that we want them in our own gardens.

Of course, this burst of new growth changes the appearance of the landscape. Many gardeners see plants and trees exceeding their boundaries as new growth pushes them into new areas. There is a strong tendency to prune, transplant and even remove plants entirely during this period, but future cultural problems can be avoided if excessive spring growth is handled with restraint. Overly-pruned plants will not bloom well the following season, and cut-

Freda Wilkins

ting too much terminal growth can create sheared appearances that don't allow some plants to achieve a natural, graceful style. Pruning no more than a third of any plant at any one time is a good rule to follow, and some plants need no pruning at all.

Moving or transplanting ornamentals, especially older plants, is not a spring task. Plants that have broken dormancy are growing rapidly with expanding root systems, and will need all of their roots to keep up the pace. Digging an established plant can remove as much as ninety percent of the root system, a loss too great for most ornamentals in spring gardens. Transplanting is a late fall or winter task. If you have a plant that is clearly in the wrong location, mark it, tend it for the spring and summer, and make plans to relocate it later in the year.

Spring always brings a flood of weeds, both to flowerbeds and lawns. The same energy that drives ornamental plants drives weeds, and it is inevitable that they will appear in the garden. It is no surprise that next to fertilizers, herbicides are the biggest sellers in lawn and garden centers. Weeds cause many problems, and have no place in healthy lawns and gardens. They extract valuable nutrients from garden soil; they rob ornamental plants of water;

and they harbor countless garden pests.

There are many ways to control weeds without the heavy use of organic or synthetic herbicides, the easiest being repeated cutting of the weeds and the use of premium mulch. It is always best to try to control weeds with these first lines of defense, and to save the commercial herbicides for tougher cases when spring moves into summer. Herbicides are usually indiscriminate plant killers, affecting good plants as well as weeds; there are many incidents of valuable plants or prized turf being killed or damaged by the indiscriminate use of herbicides. The coastal areas of the South are environmentally sensitive, and the more we protect our groundwater, the healthier our lives will be. Herbicides should always be used wisely and carefully, and only as a last resort.

Also, avoid the overuse of fertilizers. It is true that alluvial soils often need help to produce beautiful garden plants, especially vegetable crops, but don't overdo it. Plants can be "burned" or killed outright by applying the wrong amounts of fertilizers to the soil around their roots. Overfeeding creates disease problems in some plants, and excessive use of high-nitrogen fertilizers frequently causes centipedegrass decline. So-called "organic" fertilizers can be just as bad for the garden as synthetic formulas if used improperly. It is important to read the label of any commercial fertilizer carefully, and to apply it only according to instructions. Using too much can be dangerous; not using enough can be ineffective and costly.

As a general rule, water-soluble fertilizers are easier to apply and can be safer than granular formulas in many situations, but water-soluble applications often lack the full spectrum of ingredients needed to make ornamental shrubbery look its best. Overuse of water-soluble formulas can create false appearances, in that top growth and foliage may appear to be lush and healthy, while the root systems and flowering potential of the plant may be below par. Try to avoid incomplete, cheaply-made granular fertilizers that contain crushed rock filler and weed seeds. These fertilizers often lack trace elements and micronutrients, creating the need for repeated applications. Premium fertilizers cost a little more, but they usually contain everything a plant needs for optimum performance. You will generally use less of a premium grade fertilizer than a bargain brand.

Spring is the season when most of your plants are at their peak. They are not able to use fertilizers to their best advantage when they begin actively blooming. In order to get the most benefits from a commercial fertilizer, you should apply it several weeks before flowering.

Whether applying fertilizers or mulches, or simply weeding around plants, remember that the root systems of many plants are very close to the soil surface. Work with caution around plants, and avoid cultivating with implements near the bases of ornamentals, annuals, and perennials. You'll need to get rid of the weeds, but pulling them by hand or cutting them with a pair of scissors or shears may be less invasive than cultivating or uprooting large clumps.

Without doubt you'll be purchasing a few new plants for your landscape in the spring. Place them carefully, allowing adequate room for growth and expansion. You will need to know the growth habit of your plant, how tall and wide it will get at maturity, and how much it will grow in a season. If you plan for the future when you "install" your new plant, you'll avoid having to prune too much later, or possibly having to move it.

Overcrowding is a common landscaper's mistake. Planting tall shrubbery in front of windows, putting shrubs too close to the foundation of the house, and covering vents, electrical outlets, and spigots will cause you problems in the future, so in this season of purchasing and planting, make sure you plan ahead as well.

Most gardeners fear that insects and diseases will destroy at least part of their valuable landscape. Though this is certainly true in some cases, the fear may be exaggerated. Actually, insects do far less damage than we realize. Plant diseases are apt to cause a few problems in any garden, but they, too, are often over-emphasized. Most horticulturists agree that up to a twenty-percent foliage loss in a plant is acceptable, and that by the time a plant loses this quantity of leaves, nature probably has taken its course in correcting the problem.

The plant kingdom has a unique way of balancing good and bad. You might need a pesticide in the form of an insect killer or fungicide, but use it carefully and wisely, keeping in mind that insecticides often kill as many "good guys" as they do bad, and fungicides are often caustic, causing as much leaf loss as the disease itself. Organic remedies are usually safer and more friendly to the environment. In recent years, organic insecticides have been improved to the point that they are often more effective than their synthetic equivalents. Organic fungicides are readily available in most lawn and garden centers.

Good turf management means quick control of insects and diseases. Though organic remedies work quite well in the garden, lawn grasses require a different approach. They become stressed and weak when under attack, often resulting in the expensive loss of turf. For this reason, horticulturists recommend some specific branded synthetic treatments for serious lawn pests. For instance, a steady stream of soapy water may be all that's needed to eliminate aphids from some plants, but soapy water is hardly a treatment for chinch bugs or mole crickets. A solution of baking soda and water will certainly get rid of mildew on new dogwood foliage, but it will not control brown patch disease in warm-season turf.

Nonetheless, it's important to avoid the overuse of pesticides. You may need a synthetic remedy from time to time, and most gardeners rely on a few basic commercial insecticides and fungicides to control serious problems, but they also depend on organic solutions for many problems. The spring season brings both plants and animals to life. The wake-up call that rings in the garden stirs nearly every living thing, both good and bad. You'll certainly want to control the bad while encouraging the good. In a nutshell, be careful how you use pesticides in the garden. Be careful, be discriminating, and make sure you know your target before you spray it!

While there are many problems and activities to avoid in the spring garden, there are also several tasks you will want to accomplish. The most important may be balancing your garden's supply of water—the key factor in plant health and vitality, and one that needs so much attention as plants respond to warm days and nights and begin to grow and bloom.

Water is the vehicle that sends nutrients throughout the plant; it's the plant's "air conditioning" system, and a key factor in blooming. If a plant does not get enough water in the spring, it will probably have some problems later in the year. It's important to give your plants enough water to encourage good health, but without overdoing it; too much water can be as bad as not enough.

For the most part, supplying the right amount at the right time is a sim-

Michael Wolf

ple task, one that modern automatic irrigation systems have made almost effortless. Landscape plants and lawns need an inch of water a week to perform at their best. A half-inch of water every three days is probably sufficient for any plant. Some may need a little more or less, depending on the weather conditions.

Remember that irrigation systems are designed to supplement rainfall; they are not designed to be the chief source of water for the landscape. One of the best investments you can make is a simple rain gauge that will tell you how much water has been supplied, and how much you'll need to add for the week. Set your irrigation system to supply water by volume, not by time. It may take ten minutes to apply an inch of water to a particular area, or it may take much longer. Use your rain gauge and your timer to determine the amount of water your garden will need.

It is usually best to water in the early morning before the sun rises. Plants will get the water they need for the day's activities before their work begins, and there will be little waste.

Water droplets are one of the vehicles fungi use to "travel" in the garden, and the less time moisture stays on the foliage of plants, the better. Early-morning watering eliminates damp soil and wet foliage. Of course, it is simple to set irrigation systems to water between five and seven o'clock in the morning, but more difficult to manually water the garden at those hours. If you are watering by hand, try to complete all watering before the sun rises and before temperatures reach seventy-five degrees.

Plants absorb most of their water through their root systems, so watering the soil at the bases of plants is much better than spraying water over them. Most modern irrigation sprinkler heads direct the spray to plants' bases and are well suited to this task, as are soaker hoses. Water applied to the root zones of plants not only supplies this vital resource directly to the surface roots, but also places water where you want the root systems to be. Deep watering encourages deep roots, a definite advantage when water is scarce in the heat of the summer. Directing the flow of water to the roots conserves water as well; there is no point in watering the sidewalk and driveway, or spraying water into the air where it drifts or evaporates.

In an age of modern conveniences, irrigation systems save time and energy, and perform the task of watering quite well, although there is no substitute for manually watering the garden with an old-fashioned garden hose. It is usually best to water by hand, not only for the exercise, but also for the assurance that all parts of the garden get the water they need. Whether you set the sprinklers yourself, drag hoses around the yard, or simply let the automatic irrigation system do the job, the keys to watering are the same: water by volume, not by time; make sure your garden gets at least an inch of water weekly; and put the water where it counts the most—in the root zones of the plants.

One of the most important spring gardening tasks is mulching. Mulches protect plants by keeping the soil cool in hot weather, and warm in cold weather, and by preserving soil moisture. They improve the aesthetics of the landscape and reduce weed growth. In fact, a healthy layer of mulch can often prevent weeds entirely if it is refreshed during the spring season.

Mulches can be nearly any organic garden materials, although most gardeners choose pine bark or pine straw. Both materials make excellent mulches, but there are many other good choices, including yard refuse and grass clippings. As landfills become crowded and expensive to operate, bagging grass clippings and stacking them curbside for collection is a waste of excellent mulch material; used in flowerbeds, lawn grass clippings can be one of the best garden mulches.

Regardless of the material you use, it is important to apply a good, clean, dry garden mulch to flowerbeds and color gardens as soon as the weather warms in the early spring. An old mulch may contain insects that are over-wintering, and a cold, damp mulch may harbor disease. Azalea beds and other ornamental flowerbeds usually perform better if their mulches are replaced in the spring. In any case, it is important to make sure that a healthy layer of mulch is around the plants in early March.

We have mentioned the danger of overusing herbicides, but weed control in the spring garden is essential. Weeds can literally choke the life from other plants, and controlling or eliminating them should be high on the list of spring garden tasks. Nothing detracts from the appearance of the landscape more than unattractive weeds and, as has been pointed out earlier, weeds are dangerous to the health of the landscape.

As with many other garden tasks, it is easier and more productive to weed some every week, rather than trying to eliminate weeds all at once. Because most garden weeds are annuals, weeds should never be allowed to flower and set seed. Dandelions can be controlled more easily if they are not allowed to flower; common wood sorrel seeds itself quickly if it blooms; and Florida betony multiplies rapidly when it flowers. Though there are commercial weed blocks, landscape fabrics, plastic mulches, and herbicides, manual weeding is a spring garden task that should be done on a regular basis.

In addition to eliminating weeds, controlling insects and diseases is a basic part of spring gardening. Insects, caterpillars, and worms can do substantial damage to flowerbeds. Good health in the landscape can easily be achieved by being observant and controlling insects and diseases before they become major problems. Keep your garden medicine chest up-to-date and well supplied, and when you see a problem developing, get control of it quickly before it gets out of hand. Nature will often take care of minor pest invasions, but you may need to help with some quick applications of pesticides.

Though you should avoid overuse of chemical applications, allowing a beautiful garden to go to waste because of an insect or disease would be regrettable. Watch closely as your garden comes alive in the spring; along with the beauty of the season will come some subtle enemies of a healthy landscape. Control them as quickly as possible before they ruin your good efforts.

As the spring season gets underway, you will have more organic waste on hand, especially lawn clippings and hedge trimmings. Compost takes on a new importance in the spring garden, and will become a valuable addition to your landscape in many ways. It can be used to supplement color gardens, perennial beds, container-grown plants, hanging baskets and seed beds, to repair lawns, and to mix with mulch. Adding to your compost bin is a daily task in the spring, but getting the bin ready, and making sure that it is in good repair and ready for the season is a March chore.

No spring garden chore is more important than fertilizing. Though your soil should be in good shape and may be nutritionally balanced, feeding plants several weeks before they bloom is a basic part of spring gardening. Because premature fertilizing is often dangerous, you should mark the calendar well and observe blooming times for your favorite spring plants.

Having the right fertilizers in the root zones of flowering shrubs and lawn grasses at the right time will make the garden more dynamic and colorful, and certainly more vigorous. Very often, the difference between a fantastic spring garden and one that is simply average is a bag of ordinary garden fertilizer.

So, the spring is a busy season: watering is essential; mulching is very important to maintain healthy root systems; keeping weeds in check promotes cultivated good looks; and eliminating diseases and insects equals good health. Composting and fertilizing are also basic garden chores that make an obvious contribution to a beautiful landscape.

In addition to these projects, there are two other spring garden "tasks" which require less work, but are perhaps more important than those already mentioned. Be sure to spend some time in gardens other than

Freda Wilkins

your own. Things happen in other gardens that you might like to try yourself, and such ideas are often simple and easy to duplicate. Gardeners are innovative folks, and spring seems to bring out the creativity in most of us. Also, be sure to take plenty of time to enjoy your own garden. Many gardeners spend the entire spring season working so hard to create a beautiful garden that the season escapes before they can enjoy it. It is true that we spend most of our garden time and money in March, April, and May, but if we spread a little of the effort into the other nine months, the spring season can be one that we enjoy and appreciate the most.

MARCH

3/1: Lawns that were overseeded with ryegrass are fading. Do not fertilize yet. Last call for lawn grass herbicides. Composting continues. Check irrigation systems for flow and time. Last call for lawn mower repair.

3/2: Water is essential for healthy lawns and gardens. This week, begin applying one-half inch every three days, or an inch of water weekly. Prune damaged tree limbs before they sprout foliage. Last call to transplant cannas. Did you have problems with your dogwoods last summer? If so, now is a good time to spray all parts of the tree with horticultural oil spray.

3/3: Watch the weather reports; you may need to protect some plants from freezing weather. Windstorms could develop; is everything in the garden secure?

3/4: Which plants in your garden bloom in mid-spring? You'll need to fertilize them next week. Today is a good day to purchase your fertilizer.

3/5—7: Prepare annual color garden beds; make sure the soil is clean, healthy, and weed-free. Clear the vegetable garden of last season's debris. Replace wood tomato stakes. Purchase hanging basket supplies, including hardware, and purchase summer flower seeds while the selection is still good.

3/8: Good garden clean-up is essential before the spring season gets underway. Clear the garden of dead canna lily and ginger lily stems and foliage. Prune pampas grass all the way to the ground. Check the pH of your blueberries and fertilize them today with a quarter cup of 6-6-12 per foot of height. Last call to prune lantana.

3/9: Prune aucuba today. Check Leyland cypress for bagworms. Mulch the perennial flowerbeds.

3/10: Fertilize the spirea today. Check ornamental flowerbeds to make sure the mulch is clean and dry. The quince should be in bloom.

3/12: Without adequate water, most plants in the landscape will not bloom well next month.

3/13—14: Mow the lawn today and pick up the clippings. Cut it close, and rake it with a good stiff spring rake. Make sure the lawn is getting a half-inch of water every three days.

3/15: Today is the traditional freeze-free, frost-free date for coastal areas. Most indoor plants can go outside today, but watch the weather for night frosts. Tropical hibiscus plants go outside today, as well as poinsettias and Christmas cactus plants. Start summer garden seeds today. Parson's junipers need some mulching and general maintenance. Summer vegetable garden seedlings should be outside on warm days and nights.

3/16—17: Animals are more active, day and night; keep your pepper sprays on hand and watch for wild animals, especially feral cats mating in outbuildings. Check the ties and hangers for espaliered plants.

3/18: Is it too windy for some of your garden plants? If so, stake or otherwise secure them.

3/19: Water is essential; make sure the garden has enough. Today is a rose day. Fertilize them with super phosphate and a general garden fertilizer; prune them by one-third their current height; replace their mulch and make sure they have enough water. Indian hawthorns also need fertilizing today.

> **Animal Repellent**
> A basic pepper spray for repelling animals consists of eight ounces of cayenne pepper sauce, a tablespoon of dish detergent and two quarts of water, mixed and dispensed through your household sprayer.

3/20: Today is a good day for camellia care. Japonicas may still be in bloom, but you can prune them today, transplant them if needed, and perform general clean-up by raking beneath the plants and collecting spent flowers. The removal of fallen flowers is essential to avoid the spread of petal blight, a potentially fatal disease.

3/21: Today is a good day for gardenia care. Spray both the dwarfed and larger varieties with horticultural oil spray; fertilize plants with a basic garden fertilizer and a quarter-cup of super phosphate. Do not replace the mulch around the bases of the plants, but add to it if needed. If you notice a black sooty mold on the leaves, wash the plant with a steady stream of soapy water. You can transplant some perennials, especially coreopsis and rudbeckia.

3/22: A trip to the nursery today will reveal the types and names of the magnolias that are in bloom this week. Select a few for your landscape, either by color or by variety.

3/23: The season is ending for tropical fatsia, and the foliage is turning from dark green to brilliant yellow.

Freda Wilkins

3/24—26: Last call to prune freeze-damaged oleanders. Fertilize azaleas and make sure they are getting enough water. If you have had trouble in the past with azalea petal blight, spray the plants and the mulch with a basic garden fungicide today and again next week. Fertilize your buddleia (butterfly bush) today; it should bloom early next month.

3/27—28: Prune wax myrtles if they need it. Today is a good time to selectively prune forsythia and to fertilize hydrangeas.

3/27—29: Did you have bacterial wilt in your clematis vine last year? Treat the ground around your plant with a solution of a quarter cup of antiseptic mouthwash, a tablespoon of baking soda, and two quarts of water. Pour the mixture through the soil around the base of the plant.

What are Tulip Trees?

Many people refer to hybrid magnolia trees as tulip trees because their flowers resemble open tulips. Actually, Magnolia *soulangianna*, the hybrid magnolia most often called a tulip tree, has a flower that is magnolia-like, not tulip-like. Many people also refer to the yellow poplar as the tulip tree because its flower is tulip-like. Appearing along the branches of poplars in the early spring, the flower is quite attractive. The botanical name of yellow poplar is *Liriodendron tulipifera* and refers to the shape of the flower.

APRIL

4/1: Garden clean-up is essential. The application of clean, dry mulch around spring- and summer-blooming plants is a good way to start the month.

4/2: Muscadine grapes are one of the few fruits recommended for growing in the coastal South, and are a delicious fall table fruit in most areas of the South. Plan for a fall harvest today by constructing a simple grape arbor or support system designed for rambling muscadine varieties like Scuppernong. You can also plant your vines today after the supports are in place.

4/3: For best summer performance, feed your glossy abelia today with a half-cup of 0-0-22 or a low nitrogen, higher potash formula. Leafy green plants, such as aspidistra, need a shot of nitrogen today. Use an organic nitrogen formula, like tankage, or any slow-release form of nitrogen. Cottonseed meal is a good choice.

4/3: Make sure all hollies get the water they need this month.

4/6: Prune the aucuba today or tomorrow, especially if you are growing it in northern exposure or mostly shade. Remove enough top growth to balance the shape and allow for new growth to spread evenly over the top of the plant.

4/7—8: Azalea season is here. Successful blooming of these plants defines spring to many gardeners. Brown flower buds that fail to open may be freeze-damaged. Branches that will not bloom can be pruned anytime, but be very careful not to cut undamaged budded branches. Water plants from the ground up…no splashing! Rake spent flowers from beneath plants to avoid buildup of old flowers.

4/10: Fertilize buddleia and Rose of Sharon plants today with a cup of 5-10-10 and a quarter-cup of super phosphate fertilizer per plant. Your crabapple should be blooming any day now. If not, is there a problem that needs attention? Prune quince today if flowers have finished for the season, but be careful not to upset the balance of the plant.

Petal Blight Disease.
There is a difference between old or faded azalea blossoms and those affected by the deadly azalea petal blight disease. Petal blight is a fungal disease that can greatly decrease the blooming period of azaleas. Characterized by watery-looking or greasy spots on flower petals, it will spread throughout the plant and affect most of the flowers. You can prevent this disease by practicing good garden sanitation and not watering plants from the top. Old flowers, which have merely faded after a normal display, usually wilt and fall, intact, from the plant; flowers affected by petal blight just sort of "melt" to the stem.

4/11: As activity increases in the garden, the use of power tools, such as line trimmers and lawn mowers, becomes more frequent. To avoid damaging small trees, you may want to consider installing protective tree wrap around sensitive trees, such as dogwoods and small seedlings.

4/12: Camellia day! Blooming is over. Pick up spent blossoms and remove dead ones from the shrub, especially freeze-damaged flowers that have failed to open. Prune damaged or diseased branches back to green wood. Today is an ideal day for air-layering favorite plants.

4/13: Pruning the eleagnus continues this month. Kerria should be showing flowers this week. If you prune nandina this month, it will not fruit in the fall.

Fertilizer Spikes versus Granular Fertilizer Feeding.
There is no evidence that fertilizer spikes offer a better method of feeding a tree or shrub than do granular fertilizers applied at the recommended rate. In fact, granular feeding is probably better for trees and shrubs because it allows you to place the fertilizer in places where it will work best. Spikes tend to feed a plant only where they are placed.

How to Air-Layer a Camellia Plant

1. Select a branch near the center of the plant that has a straight section with a diameter about the size of a pencil.

2. Using a sterile, sharp knife, scrape away ALL the bark and green tissue just under the bark in a band around the branch one inch in length. Make sure you scrape away all green tissue until you expose white wood. Take care not to damage the white wood.

3. *Lightly* dust the scraped band with rooting hormone powder (Rootone), tapping the branch and blowing away all excess powder.

4. Pack the dusted section of the branch with damp sphagnum peat moss (available at any lawn and garden center), making sure excess water has been squeezed from the packing.

5. Seal the moss packing with aluminum foil or heavy black plastic and tape the ends with adhesive tape, making the closure secure and tight.

6. Wait for three months. Check rooting progress by squeezing the ball. You should be able to feel a large mass of roots forming along the scraped and dusted section of the branch. If rainfall has been heavy, water may have entered the closure. Squeeze to remove any excess water.

7. When the process is complete, and you are certain that a good root system has formed, cut the branch away from the main plant **below the new root ball**, expose the roots, and transfer immediately to a six- or eight-inch pot.

Michael Wolf

4/14: Pay some attention to your roses today. Some insecticide around the base of the plant is probably needed. Try Diazinon or Dursban. Clean, dry mulch is a requirement for good summer flowering. Check the plant for signs of black spot disease. Look for yellow mottling in leaves or black spots on the foliage. You may need a fungicide to help control disease. Set Japanese beetle traps today, but set them as far away as possible from any susceptible plants. Remember: their purpose is to *attract* Japanese beetles.

4/15: Lawn and turf management day. Fertilize St. Augustinegrass, Bermudagrass, and zoysiagrass with slow-release 16-4-8 formulas at the recommended rates. Make sure the lawn is dry and clean before fertilizing. Don't trust your hand or eye to measure correct amounts; use a spreader for even and balanced coverage.

4/16: Fertilize oleanders and pomegranates with a cup of 5-10-10 or 6-6-12 fertilizer today. Both plants are beginning growth cycles that will produce flowers next month.

4/17: Magnolia leaves are turning yellow and are falling. Some evergreen oaks are also losing older leaves. Because these leaves are hard to rake, you may consider letting them drop for several days so you'll only have to rake once or twice. Spring breezes can be brisk. They not only cause leaves to fall more rapidly, but can add to yard litter as well. Plan yard work accordingly.

Poison ivy control begins this week.

Your Lady Banks rose will not bloom if it is growing in too much shade or has suffered freeze damage.

Bulb Clean-Up

What should you do with your bulb foliage once the flowers are gone? Old bulb foliage can be unattractive, especially as it yellows and wilts. But that foliage is a valuable part of total bulb performance, and will play an integral part in next season's performance in bulbs designed to last for more than a year. Some gardeners get fancy with their leftover bulb foliage, painstakingly tying the floppy leaves into bows and knots or folding the old leaves into compact bunches. But bulb experts don't recommend doing anything with bulb foliage other than leaving it alone. You can always hide declining bulb leaves among other later blooming bulbs, or you can plant some annuals in the bulb garden. It is true that old bulb leaves detract from the beauty of a well-kept spring garden, but if you are interested in keeping bulbs around for several seasons, your best solution is to do nothing. This unsightliness only lasts for a few short weeks.

Poisonous Plants

Three leaflets on a single petiole characterize poison ivy. Because many poisonous plants have three leaflets, it's a good idea to handle these plants with extreme caution. Remember the old rhyme: "Leaflets three, let it be; berries white, poisonous sight."

4/18: Older fatsia leaves are beginning to fade completely. Don't cut them off the plant, but collect them as they fall. Summer bulbs are being sold in the markets. What's your pleasure for a summer bulb garden?

4/19: Don't let your forsythia wilt. It may be growing rapidly these days. Daylilies are showing some signs of green, but do not cultivate them this week. Be careful not to destroy prized perennials as you weed flowerbeds.

4/20—21: Fertilize your centipedegrass today with 5-0-15 CentipedePlus with iron. Use the application rate table on the bag. Be sure to use a spreader, not your hands. Work on your canna lilies today, clearing the older mulch away as the plants emerge for the season. Fertilize them with a handful of 5-10-10. You can prevent leaf rollers and canna insect problems by applying some DE (diatomaceous earth) to the foliage and around the bases of the plants now and again next week. (DE is one of the safest products you can use in your garden; although deadly to soft-bodied creatures, it has no effect on warm-blooded animals.)

Michael Wolf

4/22: Bald cypress trees may be shedding. Cut your ryegrass very close these days and pick it up with your vacuum or rake the yard after mowing. Do not apply any fertilizers to your lawn other than the ones recommended for your main season turf. Avoid weed killers.

4/23: Gardenia care day. Fertilize each plant with a cup of 6-6-12 and spray each plant with a dose of horticultural oil spray if you have had insect problems in the past. If you notice black, sooty foliage, spray your plants with a steady stream of warm, soapy water. Water is essential to healthy plants and good blooms in June.

How Much Water does the Lawn or Garden Really Need?
Most gardeners say that half an inch every three days or an inch weekly is enough. Measure the correct amount by volume, not by time. Running your sprinkler or irrigation system a given amount of time may supply not enough water, or may supply too much. The only way to really know if you are applying the right amount is to measure it. To accurately measure how long it takes your system to apply an inch of water, use a rain gauge set in the furthest zone of your sprinklers. Or simply use an empty tuna fish can, most of which are about an inch deep.

4/24—26: Good days for general observations. You should see some activity in your hydrangea plants. Leaves may be forming rapidly these days. You can prune your witch hazel now, and collect some of the seeds before they split if you want to propagate some new witch hazel plants. Spider lily foliage is still up. Leave it alone, even though it may be unattractive. Pittosporum may be in bloom this week.

4/27: Perennial beds are growing and showing plenty of activity. A handful of 5-10-10 scattered on the ground around the perennials every three or four square feet will give them an extra boost. You should see shasta daisies, coreopsis, pinks, verbena, and lantana beginning to grow.

Freda Wilkins

4/28: Evaluate the shape of the canopy in your small shade trees as they begin to foliate and flower. Do some of them need work?

4/29: Control invasive vines, such as wisteria, clematis, trumpet creeper, honeysuckle, and jessamine, before they create major maintenance problems later in the spring and summer.

4/30: One of the most beautiful months in the garden is coming to an end. Enjoy the day in your garden and evaluate its performance. If you have some fresh mint, try a frosty glass of mint iced tea.

MAY

5/1: What's new at the lawn and garden center? What new plants are being used for hanging baskets? Are there any new hybrids that may suit your landscape?

5/2: Hang a fern basket in a low branch of the maple tree in the front yard.

5/3: Spend some time today or tomorrow evaluating the canopy above your flowerbeds. The amount of sunlight that reaches the plants will affect how they bloom.

5/4: Houseplants should be outdoors all the time now, day and night. Bring them inside on special occasions. Keep them slightly shaded with adequate air circulation and protection from the elements.

How to Make a Hanging Basket

Hanging basket containers are sold in a number of types and styles. The basic basket is a plastic container with an attached drainage tray on the base, though there are more decorative containers. Some hanging basket containers have a webbed insert to provide for even better drainage.

The size of the basket depends on the plant you choose to grow and how large you want your basket to be. Small baskets are eight inches in diameter; the larger ones are ten and twelve inches. The wire hangers are sold separately. When you choose the basket, count the small holes on the rim of the basket so you can choose the right hanger—some have three slots for hangers, some four. Fill the basket with excellent potting soil that is loose and friable.

Nearly any plant can be grown in a hanging basket, but choose plants that have a natural trailing growth habit. Petunias, ferns, ivy, geraniums, and fuschia are typical, but don't be limited in your selections. While you can also mix plants, it's a good idea to choose plants that will have common cultural requirements. Don't over-fill the basket with soil, but make sure the media is rounded so that plants in the center will not be lower than those on the rim.

Plant from the outside first, working around the edge, and finishing in the center of the basket. Plants should be spaced to allow for future growth, but hanging baskets look best when full and thick. Use a timed-release capsule-type fertilizer and apply good organic mulch. Make sure your basket is well watered, attach the hangers, and suspend your basket in a secure place with protection from the elements, especially the wind.

5/5: It's the season for snails and slugs. They hide under rocks and boards during the day and feed on plants at night. You can prevent them from invading your garden plants with DE (diatomaceous earth).

5/6: Plant your annuals now. Bedding plants should be readily available in the markets. Fertilize your perennial flowerbeds every four to six weeks with a premium fertilizer. Keep your gardens weed-free. Stake the canna lilies if they need support. Good air circulation around flowerbeds is important.

Acclimated Houseplants
Houseplants that are acclimated are those that are grown in shaded conditions during the summer months. When they are moved indoors in the winter, they are more suited for the low light conditions of homes and are less likely to drop foliage as they change environments. You can acclimate houseplants by keeping them in shaded, cool conditions during the summer or by growing them under shade cloth.

5/7: Soft-bodied pests may become a problem as the weather warms. Watch out for spider mites, aphids, mealy bugs, white flies, and woolly aphids. A stream of soapy water will control these pests; left unchecked, they can diminish the bloom cycle of any plant. Watch for several feet of new growth from your Lady Banks rose. You may prune it today after you consider how it bloomed last month. Does it need some trimming and grooming?

Michael Wolf

The Big Eight
There are usually eight or so popular bedding plants sold in the markets, and not too many others. And within those eight, there are only a few choices of cultivated varieties. The "big eight" varies from year to year, but usually consists of chrysanthemums, pansies, geraniums, begonias, marigolds, zinnias, impatiens, and vinca. If you want anything different for your annual color garden, you will probably have to plant seeds rather than ready-to-plant transplants. The best source for new plant types and selections is the seed rack in the garden center, but catalogues also offer many more choices.

Sources of Organic Nitrogen

There are quite a few sources of organic nitrogen, most of which are slow-release. They are available in the lawn and garden center, or by mail from specialty catalogues. Bat guano is rich in nitrogen, and has become quite popular among flower growers. Coffee grounds are low in potency, but are great additions to compost. Cottonseed meal may contain pesticide residues, but is a rich source of nitrogen. Crab meal is a little lower in percentage of available nitrogen than some other sources, but it is also helpful in controlling nematodes. Fish emulsion and fishmeals are ancient forms of nitrogen for all gardens. Soybean meal is similar in nature to cottonseed meal, and tankage, the by-product of the hide tanning industry, has an average analysis of 12-2-0.

5/8: Camellias are forming stems for flowering. Keep your eye on them. Keep the line trimmer away from the main trunk, and do not prune or transplant. Daylilies may be blooming today, especially the early yellow varieties. Fertilize them this week with a handful of organic nitrogen, such as tankage, around the base of each plant.

5/9: A shot of nitrogen is good for leafy green plants such as aspidistra and aucuba. You can add a quarter-cup of Epsom salts to your fertilizer formula to increase a plant's healthy texture and color.

5/10: Last call for tip pruning and grooming kerria. Shape it only if you need to control it. Tip pruning will cause more terminal growth, but may also take away from the arching growth habit of the plant. Be careful!

5/11: Mowing the lawn becomes a regular task, in some cases every week for the remainder of the summer. How's your equipment? Are the mower blades sharp and clean?

Freda Wilkins

5/12: Southern magnolias may bloom this week. Rose plant care continues; fertilize every four weeks with a cup of 5-10-10 or 6-6-12 per plant; make sure plants are watered regularly; rake beneath plants and apply fresh mulch often to help control diseases. Maintain control of black spot disease with fungicides every ten days as needed.

5/13: Prune azaleas any day this month.

5/15: Today is a good day for a trip to the garden center or nursery to see slender deutzia, weigela, and sweet mock orange, all of which should be in bloom. If you fertilize anything today, make sure you apply the fertilizer directly to the root zones of target plants. Avoid spilling plant food into garden areas that don't need it.

5/16: Do some work on the dogwood today. Check for pinholes in the bark, which indicate borers. Look for signs of insects, diseases in the leaves and splitting bark. Apply some fresh, clean mulch. You may need to spray your tree with a basic fruit tree spray or supreme horticultural oil spray if you see pest problems.

5/19: You should have some hydrangeas by Memorial Day. If you don't see any flowers forming, consider when and how much you pruned the plant; too much cutting or pruning too late may have caused poor blooming. A light application of 6-6-12 around the daphne will help the flowers form for next winter. Maintain proper watering for your gardenia. The fertilizer that you applied last month is working well now, and you should see the results this week.

Michael Wolf

5/20: Fertilize your crepe myrtle today. Use a cup of 6-6-12 or 5-10-10 per plant, and add a quarter-cup of Epsom salts and a quarter-cup of super phosphate to each feeding. Protect your ginger lily roots as the plants begin to grow. Keep the roots cool and protected with a good layer of organic mulch.

5/24: You'll see all sorts of deals on lawn grass seeds at the lawn and garden center. Choose carefully and selectively. Seed mixes that contain annual or perennial ryegrass, heavy percentages of Bermudagrass, or large amounts of fescue and carpetgrass are usually quick fixes for bare soil and don't create a premium turf. Choose one of the seven warm-season turfs grown along the coast.

5/31: Fertilize your buddleia today with 5-10-10 to ensure summer color and healthy blooming. If you have not done so, today is last call for fertilizing the zoysiagrass and Bermudagrass lawns with 16-4-8.

Michael Wolf

"Proofing" Seeds

Some seeds have warranties, to the extent that the producer will refund the cost of your purchase if the seeds fail to germinate. Do your share by testing the viability of the lot by "proofing" them. Place a few small seeds in a Petrie dish or on a moist paper towel and allow them to germinate in a warm place. If they fail to sprout in a few days, return the seeds right away. Proofing seeds saves time and money!

Freda Wilkins

THE SUMMER GARDEN
JUNE, JULY, AUGUST, AND SEPTEMBER

Summer is a quiet season for most gardeners, even though they spend quite a bit of time maintaining their property, especially the landscape. Many of the plants that were blooming so well in the spring have stopped flowering, and are often forgotten for a while. Summer is their season for stem and foliage growth, and for root-system development, all of which are less glamorous jobs than flowering.

As they grow and develop, plants expand into new territory, and homeowners often spend time pruning and clipping shrubbery to keep it in check. These are summer chores, and if it weren't for grooming plants, the garden might not get any attention at all. The spring season brought the display for which so many coastal plants are noted, while the summer brings little appeal for most landscape ornamentals, and the attention of the gardener is elsewhere else. Here in the coastal areas of the South, summer is time for golf and boating, vacations and outdoor recreation. It's a good thing the dynamos of the spring garden need little attention in the summer; they probably wouldn't get much from landscapers with other interests.

In some cases, the plants that were so lively just a few months back are still keeping a fast pace. They send out extensive growth and may spend a few months growing aggressively. Azaleas will often add several inches of stem growth to their branches; gardenias do the same; and spireas and quinces seem to grow overnight. Forsythia and weigela expand rapidly, and viburnums enjoy a month or two of rapid growth. These plants are typical of adapted and native species of plants that have a limited blooming cycle, yet continue to have some dynamic growth habits in the summer months. The time they spend during the summer is crucial to developing plant parts, especially roots, and how they fare in the summer is directly related to how they will perform the following spring.

But not all plants are that active. The heat sends some into dormancy, and they spend their summers "on vacation," doing very little in the landscape. These plants are governed very strictly by the "cardinal temperature" rule—the rule that states that plants perform certain tasks at certain temperatures. When the temperature exceeds certain levels, some plants become dormant and, regardless of soil conditions, fertilizers, or pruning, remain that way for a period of time. Hybrid magnolias have a low cardinal temperature. Some hollies sleep during the summer. Japanese anise shrub, some azaleas, and many hedge-type evergreens grow very little during the hot summer months and, as a result, require little attention. Boxwoods that were pruned heavily in April or May will need little pruning or clipping for the next few months. Ligustrum, lorepetalum, and camellias require little, if any, attention because they occupy garden space efficiently without creating tasks for the homeowner. One of the advantages of gardening along the coast of the South is this summer dormancy, which allows gardeners to pursue interests other than landscaping.

From a cultural standpoint, it is important to take advantage of summer for those plants that do grow well in June, July, August, and September. It's equally important for those plants that do not have strong growth rates during these months to be left alone. The calendar for the summer months not only lists tasks for the summer gardener; it lists a few prohibitions.

A CHANGING LANDSCAPE

Spring was a season of short days and cool nights, fresh breezes and a few thunderstorms. As plants and trees took on foliage, they assumed different shapes and appearances, with rapidly changing colors. But the burst of growth that happened in May slows considerably in June, and by the dog days of late summer, the landscape has changed again, certainly more slowly than before, but with no less drama. Cool-season weeds are gone, and in areas of the lawn where clover and oxalis once dominated dormant lawn grass, the rich texture of warm-season turf now takes over. Shrubs that were covered with flowers are now filled out with foliage; trees with fully-developed canopies cast shadows into sections of the garden that were sunlit just a month or two ago. The landscape "smells" different; crickets and cicadas are nightly visitors; fireflies sparkle in the twilight; and vegetable gardens pop up in backyards. The hummingbirds return; porches are hung with flowering baskets; ferns and elephant ears crowd the ditches; and folks begin talking about hurricane season. Summer is truly a lazy time in the coastal South, and a remarkable season for most of the landscape and for the gardeners that maintain it.

But are there plants and gardening chores that are strictly dedicated for summer performance? To be sure there are, and in some cases they make the summer landscape more exciting than any other season.

SUMMER COLORS

The most common aspect of summer gardening is raising annual color gardens. Planted in May, they reach full spectacle in June and July. Lawn and garden centers consider bedding plants to be their number-one income producer during the late spring, and when their spring sales stop, full production in summer home gardens begins. Gardens once dominated by flowering shrubs now display beds of annuals, some in pure gardens of single types of plants, and some in dramatic mixed beds that feature vibrant color combinations. The summer garden, which features annual massed flowerbeds, is far from plain. Grown in raised beds, along walkways, in pots beside the front doors of homes, bordering driveways, in window boxes, hanging baskets, and in containers on the deck, annual bedding plants instantly replace the loss of spring flowers.

Freda Wilkins

A close second in popularity are the beds of perennial flowering plants that come alive in the summer months. Daylilies are so popular that clubs of hemorocallis growers are especially busy during the summer months when the blooming season is at its peak. Planted in residential gardens, along highway right-of-ways, and in commercial settings, the summer color of daylilies is a charming part of the hotter months. Other popular perennials, such as hostas, are great for shade gardens, and spiderwort and spiked speedwell create attractive blue color contrasts. Verbena maintains good color through late June, and after some dormancy during the hottest part of the summer, will come back to bloom profusely in the fall. There may be as many as one hundred perennial plants suitable for summer color in the coastal Southern garden.

As in other seasons, the true standard-bearers for the summer garden are the magnificent landscape plants that occupy so many settings. Oleanders bring on the season with pink, rose, or white flowers; hydrangeas add burgundy and rich blue colors, as well as dramatic creamy white blossoms. Rose of Sharon offers old-fashioned hibiscus-type flowers quite similar to their tropical cousins that bloom in containers around the patio. Pomegranates add orange color and texture; chaste tree and mimosa sport highly fragrant delicate flowers; and buddleia attracts hordes of butterflies and hummingbirds. Glossy abelia never fails to add color and vitality to any garden and, of course, the king of the summer landscape, crepe myrtle, is the most sensational of all the plants.

"Crepes" may be the easiest of all plants to grow. Not only do they grow and bloom over a long period during the summer, but they provide the color and spectacle of a well-tended landscape without intense labor. With a variety of blooming habits and colors, they can be pruned to form small shrubs, or left alone to grow into large trees. Because they are so popular as featured landscape plants, it is hard to find a garden without a few crepe myrtles.

Summer is a time for color and energy in the plant world. From trailing hanging baskets, annual color gardens, perennial flowerbeds, and lovely ornamental shrubs, to simple clematis vines wrapped around mailboxes, the summer landscape is a time for celebrating a season that encourages gardening, yet offers a season of relaxation. Some plants sleep the summer away in quiet dormancy; others bound from the warm earth with strength and vitality. The former is suitable for lazy summer days; the latter creates opportunities for gardening. By "opportunities," we mean the use of many tools, some of which are high-powered and provide those unique sounds that we associate with summer.

THE SOUNDS OF SUMMER

One thing that is almost guaranteed to flourish in the summer is your lawn. All seven of the local warm-season turfs grow so rapidly during the first week or two of June that mowing the lawn is essential. If a maintenance schedule has been followed through the year, the summer is prime time for the payoff from this effort—a high-quality turf that creates a beautiful landscape, is free from patches of dead grass, and has been maintained to the degree that it complements the rest of the landscape. Liken it to a room with an exceptionally clean carpet—a floor covering that is attractive and clean, and obviously maintained. Carpets have pests such as pet animals, muddy feet, chemical spills, stains, and any number of accidents. Lawn grass is no different. If a room in your home is to look its best, the carpet must be clean. If the "room" of your landscape is to look its best, the lawn must be attractive.

The summer growth season for lawn grass coincides with the season for outdoor activities when lawns and gardens are noticed. High visibility, an emphasis on quality appearances, and the addition of value to the landscape are all reasons to maintain the best lawn possible, and many homeowners take the job very seriously. The result is almost a compulsion to have a blue-ribbon lawn. Fertilizer sales in lawn and garden centers reach their peak in summer months, and the second leading seller is usually lawn grass pesticides, especially weed killers. Rivalries develop between neighbors, and weekends are often spent manicuring the lawn grass. In some cases, fences or other barriers are constructed for the sole purpose of stopping the spread of competing turf or of keeping some grasses from over-stepping property lines.

Under usual conditions, summer lawn care results in considerable noise from power tools. Gasoline rotary mowers have high volume output, and edgers, chipper-shredders, and line trimmers add to the din. The loudest—and perhaps most irritating—lawn tool is the gasoline-powered blower, which has the familiar hair-dryer whine, but with many times the volume.

Because most working families are free to work in the garden on the weekends, Saturday and Sunday mornings are traditional times for cranking up the lawn equipment. Unfortunately these times are also reserved for quieter family activities. Also popular is weekday lawn care—especially after work hours, when the noise from lawn-care equipment competes with study time, early evening relaxation after work, or backyard conversation.

Michael Wolf

To be sure, lawn maintenance comes at a price. Power tools have to be used, and there is no true best time for mowing the lawn or blowing it, except that the grass should be dry and truly need cutting. But there are times when simple courtesy should be extended, and good manners are always paramount. Equipment should be in good working order, mufflers intact, mower blades sharp for rapid cutting, and machines should be clean so that oily smoke is not a neighborhood nuisance. Schedule time to get the job done as quickly as possible, and use the most irritating noise-makers less frequently.

There may be too much emphasis placed on the appearance of lawn grass. The quality of the lawn often determines the quality of the entire landscape, which is unfortunate because lawn maintenance is the most labor-intensive garden chore. Horticulturists have found weeds in almost one hundred percent of home lawns. The fact that they are there is known by all, but few actually see them if the lawn is kept clean. Lawns that are a little shaggy in the summer, grass that occasionally grows out of bounds, and leaves that are used for mulch rather than scattered by power blowers can all be acceptable.

Following are some suggestions for maintaining a healthy lawn without excessive work:

1. Mow the lawn when the grass is dry and truly needs cutting.
2. Try to use a walk-behind mower when possible. You'll get a more detailed cut, and some necessary exercise!
3. Use a mulching-type mower that recycles grass clippings.
4. Use leaves, grass and yard debris in your compost pile or as mulch. Bagging the debris and stacking it curbside for garbage pick-up just adds more to landfills, and wastes a valuable source of organic material.
5. Wear old-fashioned golf shoes with spikes when you work the lawn to aerate at the same time.
6. Develop several patterns of mowing, using a different pattern each time you mow.
7. Be considerate of the neighborhood and mow at friendly times.

THE BEST MONTH OF SUMMER AND THE MEAN SEASON

You'll notice in the calendar that September is included as a summer month. In cooler areas of the country, September signals the coming of fall, but here, September is mild and pleasant, not much different from the weather in August. People who have faithfully taken care of the summer garden and lawn since early June now need a month for themselves as a reward.

Here in the coastal South, they get just that. From Labor Day until the end of September, the winds are light, the sun is bright, and the days are long enough to enjoy a myriad of outdoor hobbies. Gardening can certainly be one of those, but September is not a month crowded with tasks and challenges. Whether we are simply tired of gardening and need a break after a long summer, or whether nature puts the brake on things for a while, we are done with it for the most part, and interest subsides along with lawn and garden activity. The break won't last long; fall is fast approaching and a cool night here and there is not uncommon in this last summer month.

There are, of course, a few necessary tasks to perform during September. Fertilizing the lawn for the upcoming dormant season is important. Watering is essential, especially for fall bloomers, and so is keeping the annual flowerbeds in good order. Other than some obvious duties, though, September is a summer month devoted to the gardener, not the garden.

Since June 21st, (the Summer Solstice and the longest day of the year), the landscape has been changing. The rapid growth of many plants has slowed, flowering in many shrubs has diminished, and some plants have actually slipped into early dormancy. The budding process has been established in fruit trees, azaleas, and most early spring flowering shrubs, and there is little left for the plants to do except expand their root systems and gather strength for the winter. The landscape is quickly becoming dormant and should not be pushed to unnatural levels. Plants that have completed their processes for the year are now preparing for a different season and should be left alone. Taking a month off is not only good for you, it is essential for the lawn and garden that has performed so well for the last several months.

If there is every reason to relax, there is also a reason to keep an eye on the tropics. The 15th of September is the peak of the Atlantic hurricane season, and history indicates that no September is totally safe from stormy weather. At the least, an Atlantic low pressure system will send us indoors for a day or two; at worst we'll be pummeled by a hurricane. The calendar and the "how to" section cover hurricane preparedness extensively. While it is senseless to worry, it is important to protect your property as best you can. Plants that stand in water for long periods of heavy rain are susceptible to drowning. Those that are desiccated by high winds or damaged by salt spray suffer setbacks in September that take months to repair, regardless of how much you are able to help them. Some events can't be avoided, but the more you prepare, the less you'll have to repair when the storm is over.

The delightful days of early June, red geraniums for the Fourth of July, Queen Anne's lace and clematis vines in August and, finally, the remaining crepe myrtles of September, are all reminders of the more pleasant days of summer along the coast. The season is made for gardening, and whether we take it easy or seriously, whether we work hard on the lawn or let it go its own way, the four months from June through September can be the most rewarding, and certainly the most pleasant months of the year.

JUNE

6/1: Don't let landscape plants wilt in the heat. Caladiums and other summer bulbs should have been planted by now, and some may already be up and growing. Last call to purchase and plant gladioli if you want the best selection; don't wait for "specials" and reduced prices.

6/2: If your garden soil is dry, today is a good day for soil testing. Last call for planting summer tomatoes. Spiderwort should be blooming any day.

6/3: Water is essential. Vegetable gardens, annuals and perennials need water to grow properly. Cypress knees are not only vital to the health of cypress trees, but are also a valuable part of the landscape. Are yours exposed so they can be appreciated?

Michael Wolf

Transpiration Rates
Transpiration is the process by which water escapes the foliage of plants and becomes water vapor. On hot, windy days, a plant may transpire more water than it can absorb through its roots. To keep your plants cool without wilting, you may need to increase the protection from the sun by growing them in more shaded conditions and making sure they are mulched.

Michael Wolf

Mole Crickets

Mole crickets are strange-looking pests with enormous appetites and destructive habits. They eat all grass plant parts, including roots, stems, and foliage. They live in tunnels underground where they breed and, once mature, exit the tunnels and feed in the open lawn. They can crawl or hop and are equipped with wings for flying. Both sexes and all life stages of the insect, from infant to adult, eat plant parts. Once you notice the damage from mole crickets, they are probably already in another part of the lawn, so all areas of the lawn must be treated, especially healthy areas. It will do no good to treat sections that have already been damaged. Be quick and efficient. Stop this pest before it seriously damages—or even destroys—your fine turf. Mole crickets are especially damaging to St. Augustinegrass.

6/4: You may notice chinch bugs and mole crickets in your lawn grass. Be prepared with a basic lawn grass insecticide. Prevent serious attacks with regular applications, following the label instructions carefully.

6/5: Rugosa roses should be in full bloom with rapid foliage growth rates. Tomato care—especially watering and fertilizing—continues. Do not work around plants when they are wet. If you have not applied your main-season fertilizer for St. Augustinegrass, Bermudagrass or zoysiagrass, do it today. The formula is 16-4-8. Are you growing centipedegrass? If you have not applied your 5-0-15 CentipedePlus Brand with Iron, do so today. It's last call for feeding most warm-season turf with slow-release, one-time formulas.

6/6: Your abelia, "the workhorse of the Southern garden," is beginning to bloom. To preserve the arching growth habit of this plant, do not prune it again through the end of summer.

Taking Soft-Stem Cuttings

Before you begin, assemble all the parts and tools you will need. Use a sharp knife or razor blade for cutting. Choose a strong, healthy section of the stem that is has not wilted and is at least two inches in length. Cut it at an angle. Dip the stem in a rooting hormone powder, tap it gently with your finger to knock away excess powder and blow it off so that powder residue is not obvious. Place the cutting in an 8-ounce plastic glass filled with a mixture of half vermiculite and half perlite that is damp, but not soaking wet. Keep the foliage of the cutting misted. Watch as roots are formed. When the glass is swirling with new roots, transfer the rooted cutting to a six-inch pot filled with good potting soil.

Michael Wolf

6/7: Soft-stem cutting day. Regardless of the weather, take some cuttings from growing plants. Last call today for pruning the Lady Banks rose. If you air-layered camellias back in the spring, check them today for root formation by squeezing the mass to see if it feels firm, almost solid. Are they labeled properly?

6/8—9: Sawfly larvae may attack river birch trees. They are difficult to control, but are quite obvious as small, wiry, black worms. Birds will eat them, so try not to treat them. You can sacrifice as much as twenty percent of the foliage without damaging the health and vigor of the tree. Do you have too much canopy over your annual color garden? Will your plants be growing in too much shade?

6/10: Your buddleia should be blooming. Remove dead flower spikes and make sure the plant is watered. Blueberries should have fruit developing. If not, what happened? Late freeze? Improper pruning? No flowers?

6/11: Some annuals, especially zinnias, have rusty or mildewed foliage—the result of hybridizing to get a better flower at the expense of poor foliage. You can help the plant's appearance with a spray of one tablespoon baking soda and a dash of dish detergent mixed in a gallon of water, applied every week for three weeks. Weak foliage should not harm the plant.

Care for Hanging Baskets

Remember that hanging baskets require more water than ordinary plants because they are suspended. Air circulation dries the soil and the sun heats the container. Because the soil is confined and more water is used, the soil may become leached of nutrients. You'll probably need more fertilizer as well as more water. You can extend the life of your basket by keeping it in partial sun rather than direct sunshine, and by deadheading the hanging or trailing plants. Excessive growth can be tip-pruned to maintain balance and shape. Baskets can be protected by hanging them in low tree limbs or along the eaves of shaded porches.

Michael Wolf

6/12: Daffodil foliage should be gone now. Easter lilies should be about to bloom. Keep your fruit tree spray handy in case of disease problems in peaches, plums, and small stone fruit trees. If you prune wax myrtle from now through the fall, you'll destroy the waxy, blue berries along the branches.

6/13—15: Control weeds and vines, especially poison ivy and honeysuckle, or you'll have a problem later. Continue to mow the lawn using sharp blades and equipment that's in good running order. Fruit should be forming in the pomegranate. If not, are you growing a "double" flowering hybrid? Their flowers are sterile.

Deadheading

Removing the dead flowers atop annuals and perennials encourages the plants to set more flowers, not seeds. It is best not to do this task with scissors or shears, but by pinching out the spent flowers with your fingers. If you do a little deadheading every day, the task will be easier.

Crepe Myrtles

Crepe myrtles can be trained to develop straight branches without "knees" or large callused sections by pinching some of the new growth stems and allowing only one or two new branches to develop along the trunk. You'll have limited top-growth, but more graceful, arching branches, larger flowers, and less clustering in the tops of the shrubs.

Freda Wilkins

6/16: Prune your poinsettia today by taking one-third of the foliage off the top of the plant. Clumps of pampas grass are growing rapidly and are homes to wildlife, bees, and yellow jackets. Be careful working around them. Feral cats are mating these days; notify animal control if you have a problem. Water in the garden is essential; remember to measure it by volume, not by time.

6/17—18: Last call to prune azaleas. If you miss pruning today, you'll have to wait until next spring. You might notice some lace bugs eating the margins of azalea foliage; treat them if they are causing a major problem. Your tropical fatsia plant has all new foliage, and though it appeared to be dying, it is now rebounding quite well. Gardenias should be in full bloom today or maybe later in the week. Prune and harvest at will.

Common Insects—and Organic Solutions

Lace bugs, some beetles, and most biting insects are easily controlled with pyrethin spray, a botanical insecticide which is sold in both liquid and powder forms. Sometimes it is mixed with Rotenone, another botanical bug killer. Sucking insects, including worms and caterpillars, are best controlled with Dipel, a powder or liquid spray that is made from bacteria called *bacillus thuringiensis*. Commonly called Bt, this "gut buster" is deadly to caterpillars and worms but almost completely safe to the environment, to warm-blooded animals, and to birds. Pyrethrin spray, Rotenone powder, and Dipel dust are three organic insecticides that should always be a part of the garden medicine chest.

Freda Wilkins

6/19: Your dogwood may need some help these days. If you notice a fungal disease in the foliage, stippled leaves, mildew, deformed foliage, and an overall lethargy, try a single application of commercial fruit tree spray today. Before fertilizing, give the spray a chance to work. You can repeat the application twice more in the coming two weeks.

6/20: Deadhead the annuals. Hostas may be in bloom.

6/21: The Summer Solstice. Today is the longest day of the year. Rose care continues. How are yours performing? Do they need some general care? When did you fertilize them? Remember to treat them for disease and pest control every four weeks at least, and feed them at the same time.

Freda Wilkins

6/22: Rose of Sharon should be in bloom this week. Osmanthus will be blooming in about 90 days, so today is a good day to apply a shot of nitrogen around the base of the plant. Use bloodmeal, cottonseed meal, or tankage.

6/23: Check your junipers and Leyland cypress for bagworms. They can be knocked out of the tree with a reach pole and if you break the bags, the birds will eat the worms. Hang a few hydrangea blossoms upside down in the attic to dry. You can spray the dried flowers with hairspray to keep them from shedding.

6/24: Check your pittosporum today. It should have finished blooming and should be showing good growth. Prune by shearing it into shape, or remove selected parts to maintain the correct size. If the plant appears weak, check the pH and modify the soil around the base by maintaining slightly acid soil. Fertilize if needed with a cup of 6-6-12 or 5-10-10.

6/25: Check your hurricane preparations list today, both for the house and the garden. Walk your property with an eye on limbs and trees that need pruning or removing. Diseased, damaged or dead material needs to be cut. All fruiting hollies should have their berries. If not, did we have a late freeze? Are your plants male or female? You need at least one of each for berries, although they can be as far apart as one hundred feet. Do not prune hollies after today. Watering in the garden is essential, but do not over-water.

Freda Wilkins

6/26: Fertilize your forsythia plant with a cup of 0-0-22.

6/27: Cut some eucalyptus stems for preserving.

6/28: Oleanders should be in full bloom. Fertilize your camellias with a cup of 5-10-10 and a shot of super phosphate today.

Lawn and Garden Hurricane Season Checklist

1. Limbs that overhang the driveway, are against the house or garage, or are over the patio need some attention.
2. Prune large shrubbery that is too close to the foundation.
3. Stake or secure weak plants.
4. Secure the woodpile.
5. Create dry storage areas for garbage cans and utility containers.
6. Have a few large tarps on hand for collecting lawn and garden debris dropped in storms.
7. Prune diseased, damaged, or dead material.
8. Check the chain saw and the generator.
9. If necessary, contact an arborist for a review of your trees. Otherwise, make sure you are on the list for damage control in the event that you need a tree surgeon.
10. Make sure lawn and garden equipment—especially loppers, shears, and power tools—are in good repair.
11. Clear the ditches and ditch banks, and make sure drainage is clear and weed-free.
12. Remove piles of debris, garden refuse, and stacks of unwanted garden materials.

Preserving Stem Cuttings

New-growth foliage of many plants, including eucalyptus, can be preserved with a solution of one-third glycerin and two-thirds hot water. Cut stems of foliage early in the morning with a sharp knife or shears, and remove the foliage from the bottom third of the stem. Fill a glass vase with the glycerin solution, and place the bottom sections of the stems in the mixture. As the stems absorb the solution, replace the lost mixture with more warm water. In about four to six weeks, remove the stems from the solution. Your cuttings will be preserved for a few months, maybe longer. Much evergreen foliage can be preserved this way.

6/29: Check the shore juniper for root-rot disease, as indicated by brown foliage and brittle stems. Treat the disease with a soil drench of Daconil fungicide poured into the root system of the affected plant. Use a half-gallon of mixed fungicide per application once a week for three weeks. Magnolias are in full bloom. Maintain your perennial flowerbed, making sure it is weed-free, fertilized, and watered. Canna lilies need plenty of room to expand. Deadhead annuals and perennials.

6/30: Last call today for shaping deutzia, weigela, and mock orange shrubs. As the days get hotter and more humid, growth slows for many plants. Some summer dormancy is normal. Many plants look "sleepy." Don't expect plants to perform at peak levels when the heat is intense.

An Oily Sheen on the Leaves of Landscape Plants

This sheen is probably the result of iron bacteria that make the foliage of landscape plants appear to have an iridescent sheen, as if it had been sprayed with oil. It is common with landscape plants that are watered with untreated well water. You can solve the problem by having your water treatment company install an inexpensive device that is designed to treat water that is heavy with iron, or you can simply spray the affected plants with a one-percent household bleach and water solution.

Michael Wolf

JULY

7/1: Don't let the garden wilt. Adequate water is essential for disease resistance, good growth, and flowering. July is the month for crepe myrtles, and yours should be in bloom today. If you are using fertilizers for specific shrubs and plants, make sure you hit the target, not other plants that may not need feeding.

7/2: Soil testing continues. Take samples to the Cooperative Extension Service for accurate test results. Continue to check areas of the lawn and garden for correct pH with simple, one-time, color comparison test kits.

Repairing a Broken Garden Hose

Rather than throwing an old hose into the local landfill, you can repair a leak or a dripping connection with a few simple parts and tools. Locate the broken section or leaking part and cut it out of the hose with a pair of scissors. A new connection between the two pieces can be made with parts from the lawn and garden center. These hose repair kits contain all the parts you'll need; just make sure you get both "male" and "female" ends to complete the new connection. The new connections will attach to the old hose with screws and clamps. Work on a flat surface, such as a workbench, and don't hold the parts in your hand while you use a screwdriver; it can slip from the grooves and gouge your hand.

Repairing a leaky connection is just as simple. Follow the same procedure as repairing a leak in the line, but take the broken parts to the lawn and garden center so you'll get the right connection and correct size for the diameter of garden hose. Soap will work as an excellent lubricant to help fit parts together. Don't forget to insert the washers and o-rings to prevent leaking.

Michael Wolf

Too Much Fertilizer

Doubling up on fertilizer is a common mistake. It happens when gardeners' fertilization of specific plants coincides with general broadcast fertilizing of lawns. (Not all gardeners use one-time, slow-release feeding; some prefer several applications of more general fertilizers and formulas during each growing season. For example, you might choose 8-8-8 for your main season fertilizer, as opposed to 16-4-8.) As you broadcast 8-8-8, or any fertilizer for that matter, keep it on target. If you spread it in the root zones of some plants, and then fertilize those plants later with a specific formula, you'll be doubling the fertilizer. Be careful to apply fertilizer according to the label instructions; do not use too much; and hit the target.

7/3: Yellow foliage in your boxwood is often due to a pH imbalance. If the soil is too acid, your boxwood will have copper-colored foliage or yellow leaves. By this time of year, the plant should be green and growing, not pale and sleepy. Tomato care continues. Do your plants have enough water?

7/4: Today provides an excellent opportunity to enjoy a holiday in your well-kept and maintained garden.

Michael Wolf

Growing Tomatoes

Great-tasting tomatoes don't happen without a little effort. Water is crucial to good plant production, and as much as an inch daily is required to make well-rounded, blemish-free fruit. Water from the ground, not from the top and over plants. Use a soaker hose if possible. Tomatoes require a lot of fertilizer and should be fed with 6-6-12 fertilizer every four weeks through the growing season. Tomatoes have a low cardinal temperature, so once the temperatures climb into the 90s during the day and 70s at night, your tomato will produce fewer flowers and smaller fruits. For steady harvesting, use only organic pest controls.

The American Forest

In July of 1776, the American forest was so dense it was said that a squirrel could migrate from Maine to Florida and never touch the ground. The dominant species of hardwood tree was the American chestnut, later destroyed by a fungal disease. Most trees in the eastern deciduous forest were named and classified by botanists from Europe. These pioneers of the botanical world were amazed at the variety of trees in North America, some of which they had never seen. Oddly enough, the names of some American native trees bear the same names as those found on the European continent. If a native tree resembled a tree with which the botanists were familiar, they frequently ascribed the same name.

Michael Wolf

7/5: Some plants, such as privet hedge and eleagnus, require almost weekly pruning or shearing. If you let this task go for a week or two, you'll have trouble catching up later. Mole crickets are active in lawn grasses, and some diseases are beginning to show up as the weather becomes hotter and more humid.

Rob Gardener

7/7: This week is an excellent time to check your garden mulch, making sure that it is clean and dry. Replenish it if needed. How is your Nellie Stevens holly doing? If it's pale and weak, consider some fertilizer this week. How are your soft-stem cuttings doing? Are roots forming yet? This week is peak performance for black-eyed Susans.

Diagnosing Lawn Problems.

There are four sources of lawn problems:

1. **Cultural problems** are caused by too much or not enough fertilizer, improper mowing such as scalping sections of the lawn, cutting the grass with dull blades, mowing the lawn in the same pattern week after week, or poor maintenance habits in cultivating your turf.

2. Not as frequent are **pathogenic problems,** like diseases and insects. Insects are easily seen with a little investigation. Diseases are less easy to spot, but generally create dead zones in the lawn with some indications of fungal disorders, slimy turf, dry and brittle patches or yellowing and fading grass.

3. **Environmental disorders** kill sections of the lawn. Gasoline spills from refueling the lawn mower, herbicide drift from neighbors' yards and gardens, dog markings, sewer line breaks and septic tank discharge, water softener discharge, underground electric lines and chemical spills are all examples of environmental problems.

4. **Acts of nature** frequently create major problems, the most obvious being not enough or too much water. Lightning strikes, falling trees that uproot sections of the lawn, and hurricanes are natural events that kill sections of lawn grass and turf.

It is often hard to diagnose problems because many causes create similar effects; it's hard to tell the difference between a dead patch of the lawn caused by spilled fertilizer and a dead section of the lawn caused by disease. Be a good detective. Trace events backwards and try to find the source of the problem before you head for a broad-based pesticide. Sometimes the cause may have a simple explanation that does not require a solution other than letting nature take its course.

7/8: Some garden lethargy is OK as the season gets hotter and more humid. If you let your forsythia wilt during the summer, it will not bloom very well next spring. Blueberries are in full production. Are yours blooming? If not, what happened? Did the birds get them first?

7/9: Dogwoods will not tolerate drought or excessive fertilizer. Keep the lawn fertilizer three feet away from the root zone of these trees.

7/10—12: Three days, three events: If you are growing loquat (a wonderful tropical plant), it could use a cup of 6-6-12 around the roots. Don't forget to deadhead the annuals. You can tip-prune the osmanthus, but carefully. If you prune too much, you'll eliminate the wonderful flowers that smell so good in October.

7/13: Oleanders continue to bloom. If yours has stopped for a while, are you growing it in too much shade? Trying opening the canopy above your plant.

7/14: Middle-of-the-month chores continue today. Weeding, controlling vines—especially poison ivy—and cleaning the bird feeders should be scheduled. Fertilize your perennial flower garden today with 5-10-10, and make sure you do not "weed" juvenile perennial plants by mistake. If your foxglove is blooming, let it set seed so you'll have some plants next year. Foxglove is a biennial.

What is a "Biennial"?

Unlike annuals and perennials, biennials, such as foxglove, set flower in the second year of their plant lives. (A note of caution: foxgloves are poisonous.) They spend the first season in the garden making nice foliage plants, spend the winter in the garden just above ground, then flower and set seed in the second year. Biennials need two full growing seasons to show color. Don't weed them out thinking that they are not performing; allow them to mature on schedule. If they make flowers and seeds, remember that the seeds will produce plants that will also bloom in their second season. Here's a cultural note; keeping biennials around for several years requires mild winters, and even a quick, mild freeze will kill some garden biennials.

7/15: Fertilize your crepe myrtles today with some 6-6-12. All landscape plants, small shrubs, and trees need water. Check your fruit trees and flowering fruit trees for fungal blight, a disease that "scorches" the leaves and may turn them black. Treat the entire tree with a fruit tree spray, but wait until late this afternoon when it cools down, and isn't raining. Acorns are forming in the oaks. Berries are forming in the pyracantha, and the bush may need some support. Don't prune it; support it with some stakes and twist ties. Have you thought about training it against the wall next winter?

7/16: Some leaf loss in the saucer magnolia is OK; it's a typical problem this time of year. Watch for scale along the branches. These white or gray bumps, which have hard shells, will destroy the tree. Treat scale problems with Malathion, Dursban or Diazinon. (You may want to try insecticidal soap as a first line of control, but be sure to add some rubbing alcohol to help penetrate the shell.)

7/19: Last call today for pruning the gardenia. Rose care continues this week, with the same regimen you followed this time last month. Weigelas need a cup of 5-10-10 and some super phosphate applied around the root zone of the plant. Lawn care continues on a normal schedule. Check your mower blades, oil level, and air cleaner to ensure good operation.

7/20: Hydrangeas have slowed down a bit, and don't have as many flowers as they did a month ago.

Rob Gardener

7/24: Some perennials are in peak form today. Achillea (yarrow) is at its peak today, and your Rose of Sharon shrub should be in full bloom. This afternoon, scatter a handful of 5-10-10 around the base of the Rose of Sharon so it will stay green and lush with lots of blooms until fall. If your lantana wilts, it will not recover very well.

7/25: Review your hurricane plans list. Do you need to run the generator for a few minutes? How is your stock of fresh batteries? Today or tomorrow, check on the ginger lilies. They should be growing quickly now, with flower pods forming at the tops of the stalks. Make sure they have enough water and that they are protected with clean, cool, and dry mulch.

Hanging Baskets

Today is a good day to replace some plants in the baskets, fill in some empty holes, discard dead plants, and rotate some baskets to a different location. Keep their appearances fresh and interesting by adding some colorful summer plants to your baskets, raising or lowering their height as needed, and making sure the baskets are in good repair. Some lawn and garden centers sell interesting containers and chains for hanging baskets. You don't have to replant them; just drop your basket as an insert into the new container. Add some variety today to your hanging basket collection. Pruning or shearing petunias doesn't help them grow and bloom any better during these hot days of summer, but keeping them clipped will benefit them later in the season. Don't let your baskets get too dry. Because they are suspended, they use more water and more fertilizer.

7/29: If you treated your juniper for fungal diseases last month, check it today.

Freda Wilkins

Michael Wolf

How to Use a Garden Hoe

If you are using a garden hoe for weeding tasks, you may be suffering from a backache. You can relieve the stress on your lower back by changing your posture. Instead of bending at the waist and chopping at weeds with the blade of the hoe, change your grasp on the handle and your position. Stand straight, grasp the handle of the hoe as you would a broom and sweep it from side to side along the surface of the soil. Move your hips and shoulders together in a rhythm as you sweep along, shuffling your feet in a sidestep. The motion can be quite comfortable and somewhat like dancing as opposed to the backbreaking strain of chopping at weeds.

It helps to have a sharp hoe blade, one that has been filed; or you can change from a traditional American garden hoe to the European scuffle-type hoes that have a sharp open-faced blade. Open-faced blades allow soil and weeds to pass through the center of the hoe blade without building up in a pile.

AUGUST

8/1: August will not be a busy month for lawn and garden activities. It's a great time to make some plans for future flowerbeds, shrubbery renovations, and improvements. But planning is all that is required. Major projects should wait for cooler weather. In the meantime, don't let the garden wilt. Water is crucial for good plant growth and development.

8/2: Going on vacation this month? Make plans now to have your garden tended while you're away. Normal weekly maintenance will be required, especially bird feeding, watering, and houseplant care. Automatic watering devices are available, especially for houseplants, but in the coastal South, we face weather conditions that are unpredictable. Your best source of care is personal attention. Automatic devices are unreliable, especially if the power goes off and upsets the timer.

Fungi

Fungi are actually plants. They lack the vascular systems of typical garden plants, of course, but they live and thrive in the garden. Sometimes fungi are very noticeable: mildew on the foliage of crepe myrtles, blighting conditions in fruit trees, greasy patches in lawn grass, or open lesions in annual bedding plants. Sometimes they are less obvious: discolored sections of leaves or causing problems below the soil level in root systems. Though many fungi are bad for plants and create diseases that destroy flowers as well as plant parts, other fungi are indications of health and vitality. For instance, mushrooms are fungi and thrive in organically-rich soil.

When fungal diseases attack the garden, there are several ways to treat them. Commercial fungicides are the quickest solution. There are many from which to choose; some are synthetic, such as Daconil and Bayleton, and some are organic, such as copper sulfate, Top-Cop, and Basi-Cop. Bordeaux Mix is also a well-established organic fungicide. Another reliable remedy for many simple fungal diseases is baking soda. A simple solution of one-fourth cup baking soda and a dash of ordinary dish detergent in a gallon of water applied once a week for three weeks to diseased foliage and flowers will often solve the problem.

Of course, the best solution is always prevention. Good garden clean-up is essential, especially not letting diseased plant parts accumulate on the ground or remain on the plant, and not over-watering the garden. Fungi spread and mature in wet or damp warm environments. It's hard to change the environment of the coastal garden, but keeping a bottle of fungicide in your garden medicine chest will reduce the effects of disease in many landscape plants, particularly soft-stem plants.

8/3: The muggy days of August cause fungal problems. Be prepared to treat serious plant diseases.

8/5: Soil testing continues. Some hedges, including privet and eleagnus, need to be pruned frequently.

8/6: Hydrangeas have almost finished blooming for the season, and some of the flowers have dried naturally on the plant. You can harvest some of these "green flowers" for display in dried flower bouquets for the fall.

> **Dr. Plant's Soil Mix**
> Mix equal amounts of Baccto heavy brand potting soil, Peter's Professional potting soil, and vermiculite. The soil mix will be friable, well drained, and easy to handle.

8/7—8: Remember those soft-stem cuttings that you took several months ago? How are they doing? Are they ready for transplanting to soil mixes?

8/9: Today is the best time of the month to evaluate shade and canopy over the garden. Prune at will to open your garden to more sunlight. Replace the mulch around garden plants if needed. Japanese maples and other plants may have some damage from lace bugs that eat their foliage. Twenty-percent foliage loss is acceptable, but if there is significant damage, treat your garden plants this week with an organic insecticide like Rotenone or pyrethrin. You can collect a few gardenia cuttings today for rooting over the winter.

8/12: You can prune your Savannah holly today to maintain good shape for the coming holidays. You might lose some red berries, so be careful what you cut.

8/13: Trumpet vines are blooming in the tops of many trees; their brilliant orange flowers will attract hummingbirds. These are the famous "dog days" of summer.

8/14: As summer wanes, so do many perennial plants and summer bulbs. If you want to move them during the winter, tag or flag them today so you'll know where and what they are later.

Freda Wilkins

8/15: Mid-month chores continue today. Weeding, controlling vines, and checking poison ivy are essential tasks. Clean the bird feeders today; repair the wind chimes; and eliminate standing water around the house to help control mosquitoes. Deadheading annuals and perennials is a regular task, and you may notice some caterpillar damage. Dipel is the traditional solution for worms and caterpillars, but hand removal and relocation of caterpillars is preferable. You don't want to destroy a future tiger swallowtail!

The Dog Days

The dog days of summer are the hot, humid days of July, August, and September. The Romans associated such days with Sirius, the Dog Star, which is high in the sky during this period.

8/16: Some trees and shrubs—privet and cherry laurel, for example—are making berries and fruit this month. These berries are a valuable part of the mast (food source for wildlife), and decreased activity in the bird feeders indicates plenty of food in the garden.

8/17: Plan your fall vegetable garden today. It's too early to plant it, but get your plan and materials together. Daylilies have finished for the season, but you may notice a few late bloomers still flowering. Do not fertilize them this month. Pampas grass plumes are forming, and you can divide your three-year-old and older hostas today.

Is It Worth It?

There are plenty of horticulturists who do not raise roses in their gardens because of the time-consuming effort it takes to produce quality flowers and plants. In the coastal garden, roses are susceptible to so many diseases and pests that gardeners must tend their rose gardens almost daily. Roses are supposed to provide beauty and fragrance, and often they are quite remarkable. But raising a beautiful rose garden takes considerable time and effort, especially in the summer. Is it worth it?

8/20: Lawn mower maintenance day. Check the blades, oil level, air filter, and spark plug. Remember, safety first!

8/21: Roses need some attention today. Light pruning, watering, mulching, and pest control are chores that continue through the summer and fall.

8/24: *Clematis paniculata*, sweet autumn clematis, is in full bloom. Weedy and somewhat wild, it rambles over all types of structures and shrubbery and can take over if not properly trained. Don't miss this spectacle of late summer; if you want some for your place, now is the time to take cuttings or purchase a vine for your garden. It is highly fragrant.

8/25: Spend a few minutes today checking your hurricane supplies. Run the generator for a few minutes and check your stock of batteries and fresh water. Are you keeping the lawn and garden free from piles of debris? Today is a good day for clearing a space in the shed or garage for dry storage in case a storm comes this way.

8/28: Last call today for pruning evergreen shrubs such as pittosporum and boxwood. After today, you'll have to leave them alone for the season. Late this afternoon will be an excellent time, but not if it rains.

8/30: Feed your camellia plants today, both sasanquas and japonicas, with a cup of Sul-Po-Mag (0-0-22) applied to the root zone of each plant.

Freda Wilkins

SEPTEMBER

9/1: Lawn and garden activity increases a little this month. As summer draws to a close, the garden eases into dormancy, but there's a lot to do as you prepare for fall. Do you need some help around the garden? How about scheduling a workday for a landscape crew, or maybe a local high school or college student who can lend a hand?

9/2: Last call today for soil testing. You can still send a sample to the Cooperative Extension Service for a complete evaluation, or you can continue to test with kits purchased at the lawn and garden center. The results of the test will indicate and needed soil modification. It takes a while for modifiers to work, so plan to get that project done this month. The cannas are winding down this week. Did you have leaf rollers that diminished the blooming? Make sure you rake beneath the plants and apply clean mulch this week.

9/3: Don't let the garden wilt. Plants still need ample water during the hot days of September. Weak hollies are no good for winter display. Today is the best day for fertilizer and a cup of Epsom salts around the base of each plant to preserve dark green foliage during the holidays. Tip-prune crepe myrtles today for extra blooming this month. A shot of 5-10-10 around the bases of your ligustrum plants will darken foliage and increase vitality through the fall.

9/4: Lazy summer days may have led to some general garden neglect. Weeds may have exceeded limits, and debris may have piled up during the previous weeks. Plan a workday for general clean-up. Can you get to it today?

9/5: Today is the last day for fertilizing perennials until next spring. Annuals are fading and fertilizing them now will be wasteful. You may need their space for fall pansies. Water the *Camellia sasanquas*.

What is Dew?

The "dew point" is the temperature at which water vapor in the air changes to liquid (condensation). The dew point temperature is either the same as the air temperature, or lower than the air temperature when the humidity is one hundred percent. Dew forms when a thin layer of air at the surface is cooled below the dew point. This cooling causes dew on the surface of the garden or fog just above it. If the air temperature and the dew point are below freezing, frost forms. If large volumes of air are cooled below the dew point, clouds or heavy fog are formed.

9/6—8: A busy three days! Final pruning of houseplants, dividing, re-potting and the last application of timed-release fertilizer for the fall should be done. Use a three-month timed-release-type formula applied to the soil surface of each pot. Last call for feeding tropical hibiscus that have been blooming all summer. Prune poinsettias for the final time before the holidays, but be careful not to shear the tops. Simply remove unbalanced growth so that the red bracts will form on plants that are uniform in shape. Ginger lilies are blooming now, and you'll need to water them and make sure they are mulched. The peak of the hurricane season is merely days away. Are you ready? During this three-day period, apply the fall fertilizer formula for lawn grasses. Use 5-0-15 CentipedePlus brand for centipedegrass and 5-10-30 for all other warm-season turf. Follow the label directions carefully.

Freda Wilkins

The Best Plants for the Fall Vegetable Garden

Most home vegetable gardens are five hundred square feet or less. Though this is a small space, it is adequate for producing a table crop in all twelve months. The cool days of fall and winter are ideal for growing many salad greens and other staples that bring armloads of fresh produce to the kitchen. The long growing season actually starts in September, not in the short spring season. Plant the fall garden on or about the tenth of the month, and plan enough row space for several of these garden favorites. You may not have space for all of them, but you can pick and choose the ones you and your family will want for the next several months. All lettuces, especially the new mesclun mixes and gourmet blends (those that have several types of lettuce in a single packet), onions, late summer squash, green beans, cucumbers, mustard, kale, cabbage, broccoli, cauliflower, turnips, Hanover salad, spinach, radishes, carrots, beets, and the perennial favorite of Southern gardens, collards, can be grown in fall gardens, but they must be planted before the 15th of the month.

9/9: Divide aspidistra plants today, and apply a dose of Sul-Po-Mag (0-0-22) around the base of your Lady Banks rose. This is the season for fire ants. Be careful working in the garden, and use Dursban or Diazinon to control pesky mounds. Some plants have renewed growth as the days get a little cooler and shorter. Tag the daylilies that you want to divide next month.

9/10: Plant your fall vegetable garden today. Hollies are a prime winter plant, so help show them off by cleaning up the bases of the plants and applying some fresh mulch. Most shrubs will benefit from a late summer application of 0-0-22. Apply extra mulch to keep your plants cool during these warm days, as well as ready for the cool fall days.

9/12: Check the greenhouse and shade house for needed repairs before the storms get here. Don't be surprised to see some late flowering in a few ornamental shrubs, such as kerria or gardenias.

9/14: Many trees are changing color and may lose some foliage. Pace your raking. You'll have more to rake as the season progresses.

9/15: Mid-month chores get done today: weeding, vine control, lawn grass care, and regular garden maintenance. Notice some color change in the hydrangeas. Flowers are forming along the branches of the osmanthus; be sure to water and mulch it.

9/18: Pampas grass is in full plumage. If yours is not blooming, is it because you pruned it too much and/or late? Garden mums are readily available at the lawn and garden centers. Today is the peak of the hurricane season.

9/20: If you have not done so, apply 0-0-22 to your prized spring-flowering shade trees today. Redbuds, cherries, crabapples, and pears will bloom well next spring if they have a shot of Sul-Po-Mag today. Use one pound of fertilizer per inch of diameter of tree, measured at chest height. Today is a good day for pruning your Sargent crabapple, but be selective about the parts you cut. Too much pruning will reduce the blooming.

9/22: Rose plant care continues this month with the basics: make sure that diseases are controlled, insects are prevented from eating the foliage and flowers, and plants are well-watered and fertilized. This will probably be the last month you'll have to worry about roses for a while, but October can bring on some wonderful flowers, so what you do today will make a difference next month.

9/24: Check for pests in tropical plants. Slugs and snails, some beetles and leaf-eating caterpillars enjoy the lush foliage of many tropical plants, including fatsia and loquat.

9/25: A fall storm will cause the river birch to lose some leaves. Pine cones are falling as squirrels feed on their winged nuts, and spider lilies are blooming in the garden.

9/29: Wildflowers are in bloom throughout the region. Though spring is a traditional time for Southern wildflowers, fall offers a comparable display. The show starts this week!

Traveling Spider Lilies

Moles are the biggest cause of spider lilies migrating through our loose garden soil. Though moles, voles and field rats all share the same tunnels, only voles and field rats eat the lily bulbs. Moles push the bulbs out of the way as they move along, because their diets are strictly carnivorous. This causes spider lilies to pop up in the least expected places.

Rob Gardener

THE FALL GARDEN
OCTOBER, NOVEMBER, AND DECEMBER

Of the four seasons, fall may be the most exciting time of the year for the coastal Southern gardener. In the first place, weather is cooler, which makes gardening more comfortable. Secondly, many plants respond well to cooler weather. Plants with lower cardinal temperatures come alive in the fall season and show renewed growth and flowering. While these fall favorites bloom and grow, other plants begin the dormancy process and drift into a long winter sleep—changing color, losing foliage, and producing ripened fruit as they respond to lower light and cooler weather.

It's a colorful time for most gardens. Summer annuals still show color, although they are starting to fade, and these flowers often form the backdrop to lawns that are turning from green to brown. Those who raise perennials and wildflowers know that fall is the time of year when so many wonderful plants show the flowers they have been developing all summer. Mistflower, a delightful blue flowering plant, suddenly comes alive in the perennial garden; goldenrod bursts into bloom; and many of the native Southern wildflowers reach their peak blooming season in October and November. Sweet autumn clematis, trumpet vines, and virgin's bower, all of which flourish in the cool days of early fall cascade from trees, tumble over fences, and ramble over the tops of hedges.

It's the season for football and chrysanthemums, cookouts and collards, fall fishing and breezy sea oats along the sand dunes. Muscadine grapes, pomegranates, sweet potatoes, peanuts and homemade pear preserves are fall treats. It's time for the county fair, the start of school, open windows at night, blankets, and Indian summer. It's time for the color change in the eastern deciduous forest, day trips up to the mountains to see the spectacular show, apples, and that extra cup of hot coffee on the deck before turning in for the night. Fall brings different lighting to the garden, and it's the season that opens the canopy naturally so that plants not seen for months are suddenly exposed. Fall is a vegetable garden complete with turnips and fresh spinach, the season for last-minute crepe myrtle flowers, migrating ducks, hordes of yellow butterflies and departing hummingbirds. These three months of fall are the last hurrahs of summer for the annual landscape—their last chance to bloom, the final show for much of the garden, and the advent season for many other plants.

All in all, autumn, beginning on a warm day in early October, and ending on the last day of the calendar year, may be the most exciting time of the year. The garden calendar is crowded with all sorts of chores and tasks that will enhance the beauty of the season, and provide opportunities to appreciate it. The calendar is marked with several significant dates, those times when the garden can offer so much life and vitality. To be sure, the landscape is getting sleepy during these fall days and nights. That's what autumn is all about: celebrating the harvest as the season ends, and the cold days and nights of winter transform the face of the garden.

People who have recently moved into the coastal areas are always fascinated by the climate of this region that fits so closely against the Atlantic, the Gulf Stream, and the Piedmont. The result is a surprisingly mild climate, one that encourages outdoor activity, recreation, golf, tennis, boating, fishing, and even aquatic sports. We take advantage of these opportunities and stay active late into the fall season. If a cold night or day causes us to grab a sweater, the event is usually short-lived, and things return to normal in short order.

Lawn and garden hobbies encourage capitalizing on the moderate climate. Landscapes are redesigned, new plants "installed," whole gardens planted, garden shows are scheduled and public gardens frequently visited. It's also the perfect season to plant shrubs, small trees, and some perennials.

The fall season usually lasts for three months. At first glance, it may seem odd that I place December in the fall season rather than in winter, but after experiencing a few Decembers here in the coastal South, you'll find that freezing weather, dark and blustery days, and icy nights are anomalous. Because it's quite common not to have a freeze before Christmas, so much of the fall garden never stops growing.

Decreasing sunlight probably triggers dormancy in plants. I suspect that cool weather plays a part, but if such weather doesn't come until late December or January, it is entirely possible that plants will go into partial, rather than full, dormancy. St. Augustinegrass, for example, will turn completely brown only when the weather is quite cold. If we have a mild winter, some St. Augustine will never go into complete dormancy, but will stay partially green all year.

In cooler parts of the country, the fall season is never without a freezing night or two. In Ohio, that happens in October. In Michigan, freezes take place in September. In upstate New York, it's quite common to see thirty-two degrees well before Thanksgiving, yet the fall season there is never cut short simply because the weather gets cold. Here in the coastal South, we never cut our fall season short either; in fact, we extend it as long as we can. So long as the delightful climate we have come to enjoy remains constant, we'll classify it as fall, and push it well into December.

Fall is an ideal time for planting. Because most plants are dormant, they spend very little energy growing, and are less susceptible to problems associated with transplanting in warmer seasons, such as wilting and disease development. There is usually a good selection at most garden centers and nurseries, and prices are often reduced. Plants that are installed in the fall adapt quickly to their surroundings, and adjust to the soil long before the blooming season. By the time they bloom the following season, they appear to be part of the natural landscape.

It's also a great time to move established shrubs and plants. Plants suffer less transplant shock when they are "asleep." The cooler weather and shorter sunlight aboveground affect the top growth of a plant, but the warmer temperatures of the soil underground can often enhance root growth and development. Plants moved between Thanksgiving and Christmas are usually well adjusted and developed by spring season, and have greater potential for flower display. Therefore, autumn is the best time of the year to add plants to your landscape.

Fall is also the season for spring bulb planting. There are usually ample reminders in the lawn and garden centers, so you'll find lots of encouragement, but it's important to plant spring bulbs at the right time. Here in the coastal South, our soil temperatures stay warm for a good part of the fall, and bulbs are apt to rot, sprout too early, or fail to break dormancy properly if they are planted too early. Bulb displays in the garden centers encourage early planting and, unfortunately, if you wait until the correct time of the year to purchase spring bulbs, you'll find the selection limited. As soon as the bulb displays are up, you might consider buying your bulbs, but storing them in the refrigerator or in a cool, dry place until the middle of November when soil temperatures are better suited for bulbs.

Planting daffodils and tulips in November is an easy task, and is the one fall chore that offers the most visible results next spring. Very often daffodils blooming in the garden will surprise you long after you have forgotten that you planted them.

Focusing on the spring season yet to come and working with plants that will bloom the following year are fall tasks that occur in an active landscape. Autumn is also the season for some spectacular flowering plants, many of which are more dynamic than their spring and summer counterparts. *Camellia sasanquas and C. japonicas* are the perennial favorites. These adapted plants are so well adjusted to our climate and soil that they perform as native plants do and have become some of the most pop-

Michael Wolf

ular landscape plants. From early October through the winter, these beautiful plants bloom and thrive at a time when the garden is almost dormant. With many cultivars from which to choose, it's quite possible to have a long fall season of flowers in several colors, many of which are fragrant. Just as the C. *sasanquas* reach their peak flowering in November, the C. *japonicas* begin their show, blooming well into next spring.

Freda Wilkins

But the most spectacular event of the fall may be the color change and leaf loss in the deciduous trees. For us along the coast, that takes place long after the peak color season in the mountains and Piedmont, and can be as late as Thanksgiving or Christmas. But it takes place with all the drama you'd expect of any location, and comes as a delightful part of the mild autumn days and nights. If rainfall has been adequate, summer heat has not been extreme, and the fall storms have not stripped the foliage, you can expect a profusion of color. Tupelos, poplars and dogwoods change color first, followed by the maples, oaks, hickories, and gums—all of which drop their leaves over a long season of color change and leaf loss. In a part of the country dominated by evergreens, deciduous trees are a real treat. The show can be beautiful, especially along the winding country roads, woodland traces, and creek banks of the coastal plain. It's always an inspiring sight, and one that encourages gardeners to plant deciduous trees in the home landscape. There are quite a few cultivated varieties of shade trees that are grown for their fall color, and fall is the perfect time to select and plant those trees.

There are some wonderful advantages to living and gardening along the coast of the South in the fall. However, there are also some drawbacks and difficulties. October is traditionally dry, but can bring severe weather events; quick fall storms, even hurricanes, can rake the coast, and the nor'easters that hit during November often linger offshore for days. Cloudy, cool days with constant drizzle and periods of heavy rain and wind are typical fall weather events, and the Atlantic hurricane season continues until November. It is not uncommon to have several storms during this period, all of which threaten the landscape.

Despite the threat of bad weather, fall is an appealing time of year for coastal gardens—a season of change, to be sure, but one of moderate weather and an extended season of outdoor activity. There is much to appreciate, and many ways to enhance the garden during this delightful period. The calendar is packed with events, chores, and opportunities.

Freda Wilkins

OCTOBER

10/1: Vegetable garden clean-up is essential if you are not growing a fall garden. Make sure piles of debris and garden refuse are properly disposed of. October is a dry month; make sure the garden has adequate water. Watch for tropical storms—the season is not over.

10/2: Today is a good day to plant some garden mums. You may be able to find some sales in the local stores. Huge mum pots are popular and can be found in sizes as large as three gallons. Try simply submerging the pot in the garden without actually planting the mum itself; clean-up will be easier.

Garden Mums: Annuals or Perennials?

Mums are often sold as annuals, though in the milder regions of the South they are treated as perennials and will often last for several years. Following their first fall show, they appear in the spring as leggy, less robust, small-flowered plants. Because they have short-day requirements for blooming, they bloom in the spring, then fade in the summer, and pop up again in the fall. In the meantime, they sprout foliage, produce seedlings, take up space. If you need the garden space for other annuals in other seasons, then treat your mums as a seasonal plant only; remove them after they bloom the first time and plant another cold-season annual, such as pansies, in their place. If you have plenty of space, and want to grow mums for several seasons, treat them as perennials, fertilizing them in the fall and spring, and deadheading them as you would any perennial plant.

Michael Wolf

Chemical Growth Regulators

Some plants sold commercially have been treated with growth regulators that control their height and bloom habits. Mums are often treated, as are hydrangeas, and some other plants that are sold as off-season plants. It often takes several growing seasons for these treated plants to shake the effects of growth regulators and perform in the garden as ordinary plants.

10/3: Today is a good day to install or initiate some of the garden plans you made back in August. Begin writing your garden notes today, being specific about what happened back in the summer months with your flower and vegetable gardens. Today is the last call for applying winter fertilizer to the lawn.

10/4: Muscadine grapes are in season. A trip to the vineyard will be educational. Be sure to ask about the varieties you taste so you can grow some in your own garden.

Dr. Charles Mainland

Muscadine Grapes

These grapes are native to the coastal South. They were here when the first Europeans landed. Unlike other American grapes, they are borne in bunches, not clusters. There are a number of varieties, some of which are grown for out-of-hand eating, others for winemaking, and some for cooking. Scuppernong is probably the most famous muscadine grape, but 'Carlos' and 'Magnolia' are old favorites. Muscadines are one of the few fruits recommended for home production.

Easy to raise, fun to grow and maintain, their culture is quite simple. After the leaves fall, the vines can be harvested for home crafts, baskets, wreaths and ornaments. For best culture, prune all vines back to the previous season's two strongest vines, as grape flowers are borne on new growth, which will appear in early spring.

Ryegrass

Also called Italian rye, winter rye and annual ryegrass, the seed is actually a hybrid called *Lolium x multiflorum*. Although ryegrass is usually grown in Oregon, millions of pounds of seed are sold in the South annually. When seeded over existing lawns, it produces a green turf in the season when main lawn grasses are dormant. The application rate is moderate to heavy, depending on your needs. Normal coverage is ten to twelve pounds per thousand square feet on existing turf, and fifteen pounds per thousand square feet over bare soil. It will germinate in just a few days. Water it at the rate of a half-inch every three days, and fertilize it with 5-10-10 premium grade fertilizer every four to six weeks, beginning after the first mowing. Keep it cut with extra-sharp mower blades at a height of three inches. It's best to pick up the clippings and use them in compost heaps or mulch piles, rather than leaving them on the lawn. Keep a bag of ryegrass seed on hand for patch and repair work, and you should be able to produce a green lawn during the winter through April. Stop fertilizing in March so your rye will fade naturally and your main-season turf will reappear on schedule.

Caution: Be sure not to spread lawn grass fertilizer into the root zones of dormant landscape plants.

10/5: Today and for the next several weeks, you can overseed your lawn with winter ryegrass.

10/6: Eleagnus is in bloom. Sweet-smelling flowers will form grape-like drupes (fleshy fruits with stones) that are a valuable part of the wildlife mast.

Freda Wilkins

Changing the Color of Hydrangeas

It's easy to change the color of your summer hydrangeas, but you need to do it in the next week or so, even though hydrangeas are dormant. The color of the blossoms often "migrates" from pink, burgundy, and purple to a rich dark blue. If the soil is more acid in nature, the color of the flowers will be mostly blue. If the soil is "sweet," the flowers will be mostly pink. It is entirely possible to have pink and blue flowers on the same shrub. Check the soil pH around the plants with a simple litmus paper test. Changing the flower color usually requires adjusting the pH by a point or two either way. To make blue flowers, apply a half-cup of garden sulfur to the soil around the base of the plant and water it in. A half-cup of sulfur will usually change the pH by a point. To make pink flowers, you'll need to raise the pH by a point. That can be done with a cup of wood ashes or limestone. If you use wood ashes, mix them with sand to avoid burning the roots. It takes four to six months to gradually change the pH, so if your plant blooms on Memorial Day, plan to adjust the soil pH sometime this month.

10/8—9: Reserve two days for trips to the nursery or lawn and garden center, and for viewing some wildflowers at preserves or along the roadside in the country. Take your camera.

Freda Wilkins

Leave Wildflowers Where You Find Them!

It is illegal to take plants, flowers, seeds, or soil from the property of another without permission. Highway right-of-ways and old railroad beds are specifically included in the law. Utility lanes, timber tracts, and ditch banks are private property. State highway wildflower programs are restricted areas. Some wildflowers are endangered. Furthermore, when transplanted to other areas, some wildflowers become pests and unwanted weeds, quickly harming or even choking out other preferred species. Other wildflowers attract harmful insects. In short, there are too many risks in harvesting wildflowers. Please, for the sake of the environment and out of respect for others, leave wildflowers where you see them so that others can appreciate them and so they can be allowed to grow in natural situations.

The Most Common Fall Wildflowers

Many types of asters, which are true-blue flowers, bloom exclusively in the fall. Mistflower, or hardy ageratum, is a delicate blue flower found along the roadside and ditch banks in the fall. There are several types of goldenrod, all of which bloom in the fall, and their yellow spikes form long-lasting graceful flowers. Blamed for pollen production, they are not the cause of irritating pollen. Rather, ragweed, a noxious pollen producer, is the culprit. Morning glory vines ramble over banks and structures in October and November; rabbit tobacco has striking foliage and an interesting flower; any number of wild orchids, September liatris, several types of sunflowers, tickseed, milfoil, and gaillardia are just a few of the thousands of wildflowers that bloom throughout the coastal region in the fall. For a companion book, I recommend *Wild Flowers of North Carolina*, by William S. Justice and C. Ritchie Bell, published by The University of North Carolina Press.

10/10: Bulb displays are up in the lawn and garden center. You can purchase today for best selection, but don't plant for another month. Keep your new bulbs in a cool, dry place until mid-November.

Bulbs for Naturalizing

Spring bulbs can be "naturalized," which is to say that they will come back year after year. The old-timers planted these repeat bulbs by walking their property and simply dropping bulbs on a whim. They bloomed naturally for years, popping up in random places. Today, there are not too many bulbs sold for naturalizing. Some daffodils come back year after year, and some narcissi and crocuses naturalize, but many of the modern bulbs are hybrid crosses of the first generation and will not come back a second time. Most tulips, for example, are F-1 hybrids. Be sure to read the label on the bag or box; bulbs that will return are labeled as bulbs suitable for naturalizing.

Freda Wilkins

Bags, Boxes, or Bins?

It's tempting to buy bulbs that are pre-packaged in bags or boxes. A dozen or more bulbs in a container at a special price is usually a good value. Though damaged bulbs or bulbs with soft spots are rare in today's market because of sophisticated grading techniques and better handling, it is probably better to select your bulbs from an open bin, one at a time. You won't save any money buying this way, but you can mix colors and types, and you'll be assured that the bulbs you hand-select give you the best value for your dollar. It's never a good idea to purchase last-of-the-season closeouts and discounted, damaged goods. Two damaged bulbs for the price of one is no bargain.

10/12: Osmanthus is blooming. If yours is out in the garden where you can't appreciate its fragrance, consider moving it close to a window or door. You can move it next month when it is finished blooming or in December.

10/14: Treat for fire ants this month with Dursban or Diazinon. A fall application of 0-0-22 (Sul-Po-Mag) around the base of the dogwood tree is essential. Your dogwood should have lots of red berries that will eventually attract plenty of birds.

Michael Wolf

10/15: Sasanquas should be ready to bloom any day. The earlier varieties are already showing color. To select the right ones for your landscape, you might visit the nursery while they are blooming so you can purchase by color.

A great day for planting any containerized plant. If you have rooted cuttings that need to be planted in the landscape, today is ideal.

Freda Wilkins

Camellia Sasanqua

These plants came to the United States through the exotic port of Hoboken, New Jersey in 1790, after having been hybridized in England. They are Chinese natives, first cousin to C. *sinensis*, the plants that produce tea leaves. Early in the eighteenth century, British merchants intent on capitalizing on the popularity of English tea-drinking, sent trade missions to China to buy C. *sinensis* plants. They hoped to eliminate the Chinese middlemen and grow their own tea plants in hot houses in England. The astute Chinese, however, sold them C. *sasanqua* instead. The resulting brew was worthless, but the English developed some superb sasanquas and, subsequently, a brisk business with the newly-bred plants. They were sold to the new Americans and, although not successful in the North, they quickly became Southern favorites in our warmer climate. Today there are thousands of varieties, many of which are known only in Japan or China.

10/16—18: Quiet days in the garden. Some minor rose care continues, but you should be past the time of heavy pesticide use. Avoid further fertilizing of roses. Make sure the garden is mulched with clean, dry material. There are some yellow leaves on the gardenias as these plants lose some of last year's foliage.

Freda Wilkins

10/20: Plant some pansies today. They should be readily available in the lawn and garden centers. If you have mums in your garden for the fall, today is a good day to deadhead them.

What is Garden Humus?

Technically, garden humus is the decomposing organic matter in soil that gives it texture and rich, black color. Many gardeners today refer to garden humus as a combination of equal amounts of sand, clay, and organic matter forming the most excellent soil possible for plant growth. Lately, horticulturists have placed more emphasis on the organic content of humus, and less on clay or sand. The best source of organic matter is compost. When garden soil is rich in humus and has more sand than clay, it is said to be "friable."

10/23: On your way out this morning, pour a half-cup of Epsom salts and a half-cup of Borax around the base of each boxwood plant in the garden. You'll see the results during the winter.

Soil or Dirt?

Though the two words are often interchangeable, gardeners are quick to point out the subtle difference. Soil is the material in which we grow our gardens; dirt is the material we sweep from the floors as we clean. Gardeners "play in the soil" but never "play in the dirt."

10/25: If you want some Paper White narcissi for the holidays, today is a good day to start forcing them.

Forcing Bulbs

Most bulbs, particularly narcissi, can be "forced." Hyacinths, crocuses, jonquils, and muscari do better in soil than in rocks or water, but narcissi do well in just about any media. "Paper Whites," as they are called, have a wonderful pungency, and last for several weeks. Begin forcing them about six weeks ahead of the date you want them for display. Place several bulbs in a shallow bowl of water; some stones around the bulbs will hold them in place. Don't let the water cover the bulbs—just the bottom where the roots are forming. They can be forced in pots of garden soil by planting the bulbs an inch deep in six-inch terra cotta pots. Single bulbs will bloom when placed in the top of a vase or glass with just the bottom end of the bulb suspended over water, allowing the roots to be seen in the glass or vase. After the flowers have faded, plant the bulbs in the garden, leaving the foliage in place, where they may come back next year.

10/30: Exceptional blooming from azaleas next spring begins today. A half-cup of super phosphate around the soil of each plant will enhance the bloom potential.

Freda Wilkins

NOVEMBER

11/1: A quiet month in the garden, November is a time to watch the changing colors and approaching dormancy of the autumn landscape, while enjoying a few chores before winter arrives. Protect your daphne plants and make sure they are watered. Forsythia plants that were pruned last spring will bloom in a few months. Fertilize them today with a half-cup of super phosphate.

11/3: Good garden clean-up is essential, and making sure flowerbeds are mulched now will save some time and worry during the holidays.

11/5: Loquat plants will bloom any time. If the remainder of the season is mild, fruit will form as well. Pomegranates are ripening. Look for bright red fruits with some speckling.

11/8: Japanese camellias are beginning to bloom. Flowers and growth styles of some of the early varieties are similar to those of *C. sasanquas*. The health of the plants, color of the foliage and quality of the blooms all depend on the care you have given them for the previous six months, but remember that not every year is a good year for camellias. Some years of intense blooming are often followed by less spectacular displays.

Michael Wolf

11/10: Spend some time today in your perennial garden. As the season ends for perennial color gardens, you can begin pruning some perennials to keep their appearances neat and clean. Pruning also opens the bed for mulching and dividing plants. Be careful how much you prune. If you take more than a third from a plant, you reduce its cold hardiness. Never prune heavily without mulching heavily.

11/11: Plants that produce red berries are at their peak this week. Pyracantha, most hollies, and nandina should be fruiting heavily. You'll notice plenty of birds eating the berries.

Tropical Hibiscus Care

On November 12th, prune each branch of your hibiscus plant by one-third. The foliage may be changing color today or may be falling. Leave the plant outside on the deck or patio, but at the first sign of frost or freeze, bring it inside and place it in a protected area with low light. A garage or windowed utility room that stays cool, but above freezing all winter, is ideal. On the 18th of February, begin fertilizing your plant with water-soluble fertilizer, and expose it to as much sunlight as possible, even taking it outside on warm days. On March 15th, or as soon as danger of frost or freeze is past, place your plant outside for the remainder of the season, and fertilize on a regular schedule. It should bloom on schedule in the early summer.

11/12: Today is a good day to prepare your hibiscus, bougainvillea, and mandevilla plants for the winter. You can bring your poinsettia plant indoors for the holiday season today.

11/13: Some plants, including ligustrum, common privet hedges and eleagnus, may need to be pruned this week just to control height and density. As the days get cooler, it is normal for gardenias to have some yellow leaves; in fact as much as a third of the plant may change from green to bright yellow.

11/14: Plant your spring bulbs today. Remember to place them in locations where they will be seen from many angles. Groups of bulbs are more impressive than single bulbs. Massed plantings are effective, as are natural settings under trees and around shrubbery. Plant bulbs in a small hole twice as deep as the height of the bulb. If the bulb is two inches tall, it is planted four inches below the soil surface.

How a Bulb Works

Most bulbs spend their lives underground developing tissue, scales, or fleshy parts that supply food for different processes. At some point, they send up a flower, which is supported entirely by the food supply that has been stored in the bulb itself. Foliage that contributes to the process appears, and should be allowed to stay up as long as it is alive and green. After the leaves disappear, the bulb continues to work underground until the next spring. Phosphate fertilizer, in the form of bone meal or rock phosphate, helps develop a strong root system and healthy flowers, and is consumed by the root system of the bulb about three to six months after being applied to the soil. The best time to fertilize a bulb is before it blooms, so that the fertilizer will be timed to release its nutrients when the bulb is increasing its mass, not its flower.

The Color Change and Leaf Loss in the Eastern Deciduous Forests.
All summer, the leaves of deciduous trees have been making food and energy. The main ingredient in this process is chlorophyll, which has a green pigment. There are other ingredients in the leaves as well—chemicals that have color pigments of their own. There are yellow, red, and brown colors present, but they are not seen because, due to the activity of the chlorophyll, green is the dominant pigment. As sunlight decreases and the "engine" slows down, so does chlorophyll activity, and the green pigment becomes less obvious. We are then able to see the other colors that have been present all along. As the leaves' color changes, the "glue" that holds the leaf to the branch begins to break down, and the leaf falls to the ground. Interestingly, the color change is "true" year after year. A dogwood tree that has burgundy-colored foliage in November will always have burgundy-colored foliage; poplars will always have brilliant yellow fall foliage; maples will have the same fall colors year after year.

11/15: Deadhead pansies and mums today. Mow the lawn for the final time today, and vacuum or rake the lawn, not allowing the clippings to stay on the turf.

11/17: The autumn harvest season is at its peak this week. Besides the color change in local hardwoods, there are other visible signs of fall fruiting.

11/20: As colder weather approaches, it is not necessary to dig and store summer flowering bulbs and rootstock for the winter. Gladioli, dahlias, and cannas tolerate the mild conditions of most winters in coastal areas.

11/21: You can safely move most landscape plants today without fear of transplant shock.

11/24: Prune Rose of Sharon today.

Michael Wolf

The Autumn Harvest
Pine cones, red and green magnolia pods, pea-like pods of Eastern redbud trees, cup-shaped cones of tulip poplars, black walnuts, hickory nuts, wild rose hips, sweet gum balls, dogwood berries, acorns, persimmon fruits, Osage oranges, Indian cigars, sycamore balls, cattails, chinquapins, and tupelo fruits are all familiar fall harvests of the coastal plain's woodlands.

11/26: Peak holly season. Most hollies should be dark green with plenty of red berries. If not, did we have a late freeze last year? Laurustinus species of viburnum should be breaking dormancy this week. A half-cup of super phosphate today will encourage better flowering in January. Flower buds are forming in the witch hazel. Prune crepe myrtles today.

Michael Wolf

Pruning around Bud Eyes

Some plants have inward- and outward-facing bud eyes. These eyes will sprout next season's growth, and are particularly obvious in roses. If you want next year's growth to form on the outside of the plant, thus creating a wider spread, prune above an outward-facing eye. If you want a tighter growth habit and growth formed on the inside of the plant, prune above an inward-facing eye.

11/29: Leyland cypress makes a fine Christmas tree. Run some white lights through the branches for a holiday show and, for a lighter, more starry effect, run white lights through the branches of your dormant river birch. Do it today and avoid the holiday rush.

11/30: Prune your glossy abelia today. Transplant landscape plants today without fear of transplant shock.

Michael Wolf

How to Prune Crepe Myrtles

To produce straight trunks, few "knees," and plenty of top growth, use a saw to create a straight cut below last season's cluster of branches. The resulting new growth next spring will be from both sides of the new prune mark; allow only two or three of the strongest "leaders" to develop. Avoid multiple stems by pinching them out as the spring and summer progress.

DECEMBER

12/1: Your poinsettia should be inside for the holidays.

12/2: Apply fresh mulch to all flowerbeds and protect plants from falling debris. Review your perennial flower garden and mulch it if needed. Be careful when working around perennial plants' root systems, and remember that most perennials do not transplant well.

12/3: Check for storm damage in trees now that the foliage has dropped. You can do some limb work on your own, but contact an arborist for serious tree work.

Michael Wolf

Poinsettia Care for the Winter

Modern poinsettias are designed to stay red for a long period in ordinary house lighting. Sunny windows are best, away from direct heat sources and frosty windowpanes. Poinsettias are best kept at seventy degrees. When the holidays are over, and the plant loses its red bracts, prune it down to one-third its size. Keep it in a cool, dry place, away from direct light. On February 18th, bring it into direct sunshine and begin feeding it with water-soluble plant food. Around March 15th, or as soon as the dangers of frost and freeze are over, put the plant outside for the rest of the year. Continue to fertilize it during the off-season, keeping it in a cool, shady spot outside. Reduce the size by pruning a third of the plant in June, and tip-prune or shape the plant on Labor Day. Bring the plant inside in November for the holidays. Most modern poinsettias are designed to turn red without having to regulate the dark and light hours, so you should not have to place your plant in a closet at night.

12/4: Some plants will need to be protected from freeze damage. Avoid plastic wraps, but check your supplies of freeze protection should you need them. Using your garden notes, tag or identify plants today, especially camellias that are blooming.

12/5: Today is lawn mower storage day, power tool storage day and equipment review day. You can do these things yourself or, for best results, take your tools to a repair specialist for professional service—but do them today. The days only get busier from here. Prune hydrangeas by reducing them to one-third their existing height. (Pruning them more will mean less flowering in the summer.) As soon as a freeze kills the tops of the canna lilies, remove all dead foliage and mulch the bed with clean, dry material.

Your Garden Notebook

It's always a good idea to make a garden notebook, and now is a good time to start it. Can you recall what happened in the spring and summer? What were your successes and failures? What was the weather like during the summer months? Did you grow the best tomatoes ever? When did your annuals show you their best performance? All these questions are easily answered, but it's best to keep a record of gardening events as they take place, rather than trying to recall them months later. In addition, weather events, varieties, changes in the garden structure, special events, tool performance, visitors and guests, blooming habits, and remarkable notes are worth writing down, in your own journal. A simple spiral-bound notebook will do, and remember that you are not writing for publication. Keep your notes handy so you can review them as needed.

12/6: Deep dormancy makes plants look completely dead. Deutzia, weigela, and forsythia plants may not give any indication of plant life, but don't be misled. You can transplant them today, but do not prune!

12/8: A good day for tree work. Many trees have no foliage, so you can eliminate any diseased, damaged, or dead wood. Be careful how much you prune fruit trees. Any wood taken away now will eliminate fruit-making later.

12/9: You can safely prune roses for the season. This is the last chore for rose care for the winter. Reduce them by one-half their existing height, but be careful! Some species roses and a few antique roses bloom on current growth, so pruning may eliminate some flowering. It's best to know the type of rose before you prune. Last call for garden clean-up today. Get it done before the holidays.

12/10: Some foliage makes excellent holiday greenery designs and bouquets. Boxwood, wax myrtle, magnolia, Leyland cypress, nandina, holly, and cleyera all make long-lasting seasonal decorations and can be placed in or out of water.

12/15: As the holiday season gets underway and friends visit, make sure your landscape looks its best. Don't let shredded pampas grass plumes blow through the yard. Rake leaves from the yard and garden and remove piles of debris.

12/16: Though most folks do not winterize irrigation systems in milder climates, today is a good day to make sure your system is in working order for the winter. If you're planning a vacation over the holidays, plan for freeze protection should the nights get colder than thirty-two degrees.

12/18: Wrap up lawn and garden projects today so that you can enjoy more important activities during the holidays.

12/21: The Winter Solstice: the sun is over the Tropic of Capricorn. Today is the shortest day of the year.

12/30. Today is a good day to bring some spring flowering branches indoors for forcing. The very early bloomers—for example, quince and flowering almond—can be forced into bloom a few weeks early. Cut budded branches long and deep and place them in vases filled with warm water. Sunny exposure hastens flowering.

Freda Wilkins

Make Your Christmas Tree Last Longer

You can extend the life of your fresh Christmas tree by as much as two weeks by using the following solution in the stand in place of water: Add a half-cup of sugar and a half-cup of lemon juice to a gallon of water and stir in a tablespoon of baking soda. Use this solution each time you add water to the container.

THE WINTER GARDEN
JANUARY AND FEBRUARY

Winter in the coastal garden is a distinct, short season. It comes slowly, leaves quickly, and is with us for only a few months. By January, the days are short and cool, and the nights are sometimes at or near freezing. January is the coldest month of the year, but by the end of the month, the temperatures have already begun to moderate. By January 20th, the average temperatures begin to rise slowly, so that just thirty days later, by the end of February, there is a marked difference in the duration of nighttime chill hours.

By the North's standards, winter does not exist in the coastal Southeast. Most of the days are above freezing, and many are warm enough for us to wear light clothing. Garden tasks that are reserved for spring in areas north and west of the coast are frequently done in January and February, the two months of winter. Transplanting shrubs, moving trees, garden renovations, and pruning some shrubs are quite common winter tasks here. It rarely gets so cold that the garden suffers extreme damage.

As in any season, it helps to watch the weather forecasts to be prepared for the extremes. Overall, you can expect mild weather to the point that freezing temperatures at night are often followed by balmy days, and cold snaps are short-lived.

But the coastal gardening community is not always free from winter storms. Offshore lows that connect with Arctic blasts can dust the area with snow or ice, and even though these storms are brief, they can cause some problems in the garden. Freeze damage is infrequent, but when it causes bark-splitting and cell-bursting, the resulting damage to plants usually requires some heavy pruning to remove damaged and dead material. Ground freezing is a serious problem should it happen. If temperatures are so cold that the ground freezes, you should protect valuable plants. If the root systems of plants freeze, the plant will be lost.

"Cold hardiness" is a term horticulturists use to measure a plant's resistance to damage because of cold weather, or its ability to survive cold weather. According to many gardeners, we live in USDA Hardiness Zone 8, which means that our average minimum temperatures do not go below twenty degrees. In some sections of coastal South Carolina, the temperatures are even milder, and in Zone 9, the average minimum is 30 degrees. We can grow quite a few plants here that have limited cold hardiness, including tropical palms, loquats, fatsia, and oleanders.

Though these plants are subject to freeze damage, they often go years without suffering any. More often than not, the typical winter is filled with balmy days and mild nights. Daffodils frequently bloom in January, and flowering Japanese apricots show flowers in February. Though most deciduous trees have lost their leaves by New Year's Day, viburnums often have flowers, a few odd azaleas may show some color, and some classic favorites like

97

winter honeysuckle and star magnolia can bloom anytime in February. In the perennial garden, verbena comes alive, daylily fans begin to grow above ground, and pansies are in full bloom.

The winter skyline is usually stark and bare. Trees without foliage often show prominent buds, but leaves are not visible on the maples and oaks, and the blue winter sky is a sharp contrast to the green tops of native pines.

Winter is no twilight zone here. It is a remarkable time of year when most everything in the garden is quiet and dormant, yet some things respond quickly to a few days of warm sunshine. When we see flowers and plants appearing to bloom out of season in January and February, remember that winter in the coastal garden is mild by nature. Freezing temperatures are rare after the first few days in March, and we are usually frost-free after March 15th.

Michael Wolf

Some typical winter protection measures that are taken in colder areas of the country are simply not necessary here. Wrapping plants with heavy plastic, spraying shrubs with anti-desiccants, and storing the garden hoses aren't good ideas. Plants, lawn grasses, and shrubs need water, even in the winter, and wrapping plants prevents air circulation and can lead to over-heating in the warm days that follow cold weather.

We seldom have to dig and store summer bulbs and tubers here. Southern garden classics like cannas, gladioli and lilies are quite comfortable in the cool soils of winter, and actually benefit from their time in the winter garden. Be careful how deeply you prune some plants, especially roses, which get off to a quick start in the spring. If some plants are pruned too heavily in the winter, they spend considerable time making foliage and stem growth in the early spring, and if the spring and summer seasons generate above-average heat, they may fail to bloom properly in their flowering seasons. Light dormant pruning is ideal for plants that bloom after the second week in June, but avoid taking plants down to the soil line.

But if you avoid some typical cold weather practices, you might enjoy some of the activities that are not usually done in colder places. English ivy, for example, thrives in cool weather, and makes a fine hanging basket material for the front porch or deck, even in the coolest time of the year. Culinary herbs, including rosemary and thyme, can be lightly fertilized and encouraged to grow in January and February. Some blooming plants make ideal potted plants for the deck and patio; pansies can be grown in containers; mums that have been tip-pruned are ideal for containers on porch steps and along the sidewalk; and a deep-dish planter will easily support lettuces and chives for salad bowls.

Houseplants can spend most days outside in the cool sunshine and open air. Make sure you open the greenhouse on balmy days to keep the air moving and prevent disease and insect damage.

If winter is a season for watching and waiting for spring, looking through catalogues and planning the spring and summer garden, it is also a season for enjoying the garden with its surprises and delightful sights and smells. The cold days and nights are often short and sweet, and can be quite pleasant.

Michael Wolf

JANUARY

1/1: See some seeds in the catalogue you'd like to have for the spring and summer? Order them this week. Monthly feeding of pansies is due today. Keep an eye on the weather...freeze warnings mean plant protection.

1/2: Check the houseplants for insects. Make sure the plants have enough water. Rotate houseplants outside if the weather permits, and wash them with the hose.

Dr. Plant's House Plant Insecticide

1 Tbs. baking soda
1 Tbs. flea and tick shampoo
1 Tbs. ammonia
1 tsp. rubbing alcohol
1 gallon of water
 Spray plants at ten-day intervals with up to three applications.

1/3: Winter daphne should be budding this week.

1/4: Monthly weeding of the perennial flowerbeds continues this week, especially to control of chickweed and henbit. Clean the bird feeders.

1/5—6: Greenhouse plants need water.

1/7: Prune freeze damage in oleanders.

1/8: Replace the mulch in ornamental flowerbeds this week. Rake away all old, damp mulch, and replace it with clean, dry material.

1/9: Take a look at the hibiscus plants you are storing in the garage. How are they doing?

1/10: Last call for spring bulbs today. Plant daffodils and tulips for late spring flowering.

1/11: Draw some plans for the late spring and summer garden.

1/12: A good day to bring in some branches for forcing. Try forsythia, quince, and fruit trees.

1/13: Aerate the lawn this week by walking the entire lawn with golf spikes or shoes made for aeration. Apply one-half inch of finished compost over the entire lawn. Water it well, and allow the compost to "melt" into the lawn.

How to Force Spring Branches
Cut long branches of shrubs that bloom in early spring—those with flower buds forming along the lengths of the stems. Place them in deep glass vases filled with warm water and an aspirin tablet. A tabletop next to a window will force flowers in a week or two.

1/14: Harvest a few camellias today for display indoors. Cut long stems with several buds and open flowers.

1/15: Prune dead or damaged limbs from shade trees today. Be careful not to prune too much, and avoid pruning trees that bloom in early spring.

1/16—17: How's the annual ryegrass doing? If it's pale, fertilize today with ten pounds of 5-10-10 fertilizer per thousand square feet. Make sure you put a half-inch of water on the lawn every four days. Your ryegrass should be mowed to three inches in height.

1/18: Prune your pampas grass today. You can reduce it to the ground if you choose, or to as little as one-third its height.

1/19—21: Good days for moving ginger lilies. Dig some of the roots and give them to friends. Prune lantana this week, but no more than one-third of its growth should be removed.

1/22: Lightly prune your blueberry bushes today. Be careful how much you cut away. The fruit you will enjoy in a few months is produced on last summer's growth, but old plants need some pruning to encourage new growth next spring.

Freda Wilkins

101

1/23: Crowded spiderwort beds and spiked speedwell plants can be moved today. Relocate them to better positions in the perennial flowerbed.

1/24: Prune the perennial clematis vines this week, but to no less than 16 inches above the ground. Look carefully and locate old runners, tracing them back to the ground.

1/25: Last call for transplanting or moving spring flowering shrubs, especially azaleas. Today is a good time to transplant coreopsis and daisies, but it may be difficult to locate them in the dormant garden.

1/26—28: Prepare the spring vegetable garden by mowing the area, tilling and cultivating. Be sure to rake and level the garden after you till it. This period is a good time to renovate daylily beds by weeding and applying good garden mulch.

1/29—30: Flower buds are forming along the branches of forsythia, deutzia, and spirea. If you don't see obvious swelling in the bud eyes, make sure the branches are alive by scratching into the bark and finding some green tissue just under the surface.

1/31: Turn on the garden and lawn irrigation system today; check to make sure all outlets are working and check the line for leaks. Apply super phosphate to the soil around the base of the weigela and prune away old, scraggly branches. Reach deep into the center and use sharp shears.

Clean Tools are Important

Dirty tools spread disease. Keep your shears clean by wiping the blades with a ten-percent bleach solution after every cut.

Michael Wolf

FEBRUARY

2/1: Have you ordered your seeds from the catalogue yet? Watch the weather reports for freeze forecasts.

2/2: What's new for spring gardening at the lawn and garden center?

2/3: Check the houseplants for insects and excessive dust buildup. Use warm soapy water to clean leaves, and increase the humidity around your houseplants by boiling some water for pasta or tea.

2/4: Monthly weeding of the perennial beds continues this week.

2/5—6: Add three cubic feet of good garden compost to every hundred square feet of vegetable garden space. Cultivate it into the top ten inches of the soil; rake and level the bed.

2/7: Are there any garden shows, workshops, or seminars scheduled for this month? Check with the Cooperative Extension Service and local Master Gardener organizations.

2/8: Primrose plants are available at the local garden centers and nurseries.

2/9: Call your favorite greenhouse or nursery and reserve some specialty spring plants and hanging baskets.

2/10: Fertilize pecan trees today with any specialty blend made for nut trees, or by adding a pound of zinc sulfate to twenty pounds of 8-8-8 fertilizer.

> ### How Much Fertilizer to Use for a Tree
> Use one pound of fertilizer for every inch diameter of tree measured at chest height. Apply it in a three-foot wide band around the drip line of the tree, walk it into the ground with your golf spikes and water it well.

2/11: Get your supplies today for starting seeds indoors. You'll need "jiffy squares," peat pots, seed-starting soil mix, trays for holding the peat pots or cups, watering devices, and the seeds. There are several types of small seed dispensers that feature a tube and plunger device. They are ideal for placing a few small seeds in a container or seed flat. Ask at the lawn and garden center for a "tiny-seed sowing device."

Horticultural Oil Sprays are sold in several grades

The traditional heavier oils are used during the dormant season on branches, stems, and trunks of trees to control insects that are over-wintering in the bark. Dormant oil is effective in killing eggs of some insects. Modern, lighter grades of horticultural oil are thinner and can be applied to plants that are in full leaf. These lighter grades of oil are good for controlling insects in plants that are in season. Sold as "all-purpose" or "all-season" oils, they are not toxic to warm-blooded animals, and pose little threat to the environment. Oil sprays should never be applied to plants that are in full leaf when the soil is dry, because the plant will need to absorb plenty of moisture to help the oil evaporate after it has done its job. Heavy oils clog the pores of the leaves, so the lighter grade oil, the better. Follow label instructions carefully.

2/12: Prune the buddleia today, and apply a cup of super phosphate to the soil around the base of the gardenia plant.

2/13: Start seeds today for the vegetable garden and annual flowerbed. Watch for freezing weather that might threaten the spirea plants.

2/14: A good day to spray the dogwoods with horticultural oil spray. Check for budding in the branches, and prune away any dead wood that will not bear flowers in the spring.

2/15: Water-soluble fertilizer feeding begins today for tropical hibiscus plants that have been kept over the winter. Bring them into as much sunshine as possible. Apply super phosphate to the Indian hawthorns, and spray the rabbiteye blueberries with horticultural oil spray.

2/16: Clean the bases of rose bushes today by removing the old mulch and replacing it with clean, dry material. Perennial verbena may show some blossoming today.

2/17: Copper-colored foliage in some plants is a normal sign of dormancy. Gardenias, azaleas, sasanquas, oleanders, and even some hollies can have pale and weak foliage. Watch the weather; you may need to protect plants from freezing winds.

2/18—20: Check your garden medicine chest. How's your stock? Are your pesticides up-to-date? Do you need to dispose of any chemicals?

2/21: Prune your Rose of Sharon today, removing only unwanted stems and branches. Too much pruning destroys the graceful shape of the plant. Have you noticed that the berries in your hollies are disappearing? Birds may be actively feeding this week.

2/22: Today is a good time to prune your rose bushes, but do so lightly. Heavy pruning has no real advantage.

2/23: Apply horticultural oil spray to fig trees and Japanese maples.

2/24: Saucer magnolias and star magnolias might be flowering this week.

2/25: Replace the mulch beneath azalea plants today, using clean dry mulch. Pine bark shred or nuggets are ideal. Feed the plants with a half-cup of super phosphate.

2/26—27: Lawn mower start-up days. Using fresh gas and a new spark plug, start your engine and check it for good running condition. Mow the lawn, collecting as much debris as possible; rake it and level any low spots, using a mixture of half sharp sand (the yellow builder's sand used on construction sites) and half commercial compost.

2/28: Apply lawn grass herbicides today through your hose-end sprayer. Read the label instructions carefully and use a "dedicated" herbicide sprayer, one that will be used only for dispensing lawn grass weed killers.

Freda Wilkins

"HOW TO DO IT"

PRUNING, PART I

WHAT? Small shrubs.

WHO? You can do this project yourself, or you can hire a landscaper or lawn and garden maintenance company experienced in pruning. Avoid hiring people who have no experience using pruning equipment.

WHEN? Shrubs that bloom in early to mid-spring, including azaleas, forsythia, quince, gardenias, weigela, and hybrid magnolias, are pruned as soon as they finish blooming. Wait no longer than two weeks. A general rule is that plants that bloom before June 30th should be pruned as soon as they finish blooming.

Some mid- to late-spring and summer bloomers—crepe myrtle, Rose of Sharon, and glossy abelia, for example—are pruned as soon as they become dormant in the fall or early winter. If the plant blooms after June 30th, prune it in November, December or January.

These rules are not hard and fast and there are some exceptions. Whenever you prune you run the risk of cutting out bloom potential, but anything that is dead, damaged, or diseased should be pruned regardless of the season. Unwanted growth, or growth that impedes traffic or poses an obstacle, should also be pruned at any time, and some evergreen hedges that have repeated, rapid growth cycles—such as privet, eleagnus, and ligustrum—can be pruned at will during the growing season.

Michael Wolf

WHY? Prune to control growth and size, but remember that pruning does not change a plant's growth habit. If a plant tends to grow with arching, graceful branches, pruning it will not change the structure, merely the size. You can avoid some pruning by making sure that plants are placed properly. If they are planted too close to the foundation of your house, for example, chances are good they will need pruning. Some plants need pruning to encourage blooming.

WHERE? You can prune individual stems, entire sections, or just some foliage. In any case, prune plants by no more than a third at any time. Reducing their top or side growth more than that limits their ability to flower or recover from major cutting. Some plants never fully recover from major pruning.

HOW? There are several ways to prune. You can choose to cut selected stems, branches, or parts with a pair of hand shears, of which there are two types. Anvil shears have a set of "jaws" that closes together on a level "anvil," cutting the material. The blade closes against the anvil. The other type is called "side cutting" or "by-pass" shears. Both jaws are sharpened blades that pass each other as they cut through the material.

Michael Wolf

In selective pruning, choose individual stems carefully and use shears to cut one stem at a time. You can choose to "lop" large branches with long-handled loppers—which are heavy-duty shears with long handles. Reach deep into the interior of the plant and remove whole sections if needed.

Shearing requires manual long-bladed shears or powered shears to cut foliage and stems from the tops and sides of plants, forming a definite shape. This technique is good for shaping hedges and for individual plants that need growth regulation.

Prune early in the day before the sun gets hot and make sure your tools are clean and sharp. For sensitive plants that are susceptible to disease, or if pruning diseased material, spray your tools frequently with a ten-percent household bleach solution.

❧ **DR. PLANT SAYS:** Spread a tarp on the ground close to your project. It will make clean-up and collection much faster and is easier than raking into plastic lawn bags.

PRUNING, PART II

WHAT? Large shrubs and small trees.

WHO? You can do this project yourself, or hire a professional arborist or tree expert, or a properly trained professional lawn and garden maintenance specialist. If you hire someone, make sure the contractor has proper insurance and licensing.

WHEN? The same rules that apply to smaller plants also apply to large shrubs and small trees. With the exception of some fruit trees, you'll need to be aware of when the plant flowers. Fruit trees, including pears and peaches, produce fruit on various types of growth, usually wood that has grown and matured in the previous season, and will make the fruit-producing flowers on these branches. Obviously, if these branches are cut away, you will have limited fruit. Some pruning is always necessary; just be careful of the amount you prune. Some small fruit trees have specialized pruning requirements. Because it's always best to know specifics before you begin cutting, you may want to contact your local Cooperative Extension Service or Master Gardeners Association.

WHY? Prune to control growth and size. The same rules regarding size that apply to small shrubs also apply to larger shrubs.

Michael Wolf

WHERE? Follow the same guidelines as you followed for pruning small shrubs, remembering to remove no more than one-third of the plant at any one time.

HOW? Removing larger branches and small limbs might require a saw or powered chain saw. *There are two basic rules to consider: any branch or limb that has a diameter greater than fourteen inches, or one that exceeds the length of the saw blade, should be referred to a professional; and never use a step-ladder or extension ladder while using a chain saw, handsaw or pole saw.*

Folding handsaws usually have a row of teeth that are sharp on both sides of each tooth so that the saw cuts on both the "push" and the "pull." Saws quickly cut small limbs and branches. To cut wood easily, use the "drop cut" method, which is a series of three cuts. The first cut is an upward cut from the bottom of the stock six inches from the main trunk. Cut almost halfway through the branch. The second cut is between the first cut and the main trunk, downward from the top of the stock. This second cut goes all the way through the stock. As the blade gets close to the other side, the limb or branch will snap away cleanly at the site of the first cut, falling clear without splitting, binding the saw blade, or tearing bark. The third cut is closer to the trunk and removes the stub. Remember to use safety glasses and gloves.

Loppers are great for branches of one or two inches in diameter. The new ratchet-type loppers have a levered action at the blade that reduces strain on your wrist and arm.

Pole saws are rather expensive tools for homeowners to purchase, especially if they will have limited use. They can easily be rented, and are quite simple to operate. They usually have a lopper attachment at the head, operated by a rope on a pulley. Use caution when cutting branches overhead, and remember that the lopper will only cut branches in relation to your strength and pull on the rope. Nothing is more frustrating than binding a pole saw in an overhead limb because the loppers will not pass through the branch or disengage when you release the rope.

The saw attachment on the pole has several wing nuts for tightening and, like most pruning saws, has teeth that are sharp on both sides. Remember to stand on steady ground, balance yourself securely, and never lean into your work while using a pole saw. Because you have to look up at your work, you'll need a pair of safety glasses to prevent sawdust and litter from getting into your eyes. Use a pole saw just as you would a handsaw.

Safety first! Always know your limits and the tool's limits. Unless you are certain that you can complete the project safely and quickly with your own tools, hire a professional to do it for you.

❦ **DR. PLANT SAYS:** Saw a little, haul a little. Don't accumulate large piles of debris, but saw for a while and haul your debris for a while. Pace yourself through the entire project so that one part of the job doesn't get onerous.

SOLARIZING GARDEN SOIL

WHAT? Solarizing flowerbeds or vegetable gardens "cooks" the soil, almost sterilizing it. Once solarized, soil contains few, if any, weed seeds and is free from many plant diseases, especially the fungal disorders that destroy young spring seedlings in annual color gardens.

WHO? You can do this job yourself, or supervise your lawn and garden maintenance person.

WHEN? To generate the correct heat, you'll have to do this project in spring and summer. Allow sixteen weeks for best effects.

WHY? You'll never have to fight tomato wilt disease, damping off diseases, or excessive weeds in flowerbeds or vegetable gardens that have been solarized.

HOW? Assemble all your tools and equipment before beginning the project. Clear, rake, and level the garden area. Cultivate it as deeply as possible, down to a depth of eighteen inches if you can. Soak the entire project area with water to a depth of twelve inches. This procedure may take some time, so plan on overnight watering if necessary. Cover the project area with clear four or six mil ultraviolet ray-inhibitive plastic sheeting, securing the sides and ends in a soil-covered trench, or with some type of weighted material that will not allow the sheet to escape in windy weather. Leave the sheet in place for at least twelve weeks or up to sixteen weeks, allowing as much heat as possible to build up under the sheet. When you remove the sheet for planting the area, cultivate as little as possible. It's best to seed or plant the area without tilling. The plastic sheeting is inexpensive and is easy to find at any hardware store or garden center.

❦ **DR. PLANT SAYS:** Solarizing destroys most living organisms in the soil, including beneficial ones. Adding some finished compost to the treated area will greatly enhance health and vigor, but make sure your compost is clean and weed-free so you won't defeat the purpose of solarizing.

CONSTRUCTING A RAISED BED

WHAT? This project makes a flowerbed or small vegetable garden that is raised above ground level, contains an excellent soil mixture, and is braced and supported around the perimeters.

WHO? This is a project that you can do yourself. You can also choose to supervise a few laborers as they complete the job.

WHEN? It is best to complete the project in the late winter before the spring garden season gets underway, or in the late summer before the fall season arrives. Avoid the hottest days of summer to work on this project.

Michael Wolf

WHY? Raised flowerbeds or vegetable gardens make ideal growing situations for a number of reasons. The beds are easily seen, not only from the house, but from the general neighborhood as well. Annuals and perennials growing in raised beds create more of a "show," because they are above street level. Bending and stooping over flowerbeds is reduced, and thus the strain on your lower back and knees is less. Weeding is easier; care and maintenance of the flowerbed or garden is simpler. Because the soil mixture in the bed is above ground level, and is not the same as the existing soil, you can actually create an ideal growing environment. Weeds are few, if any, and pest control is minor. Raised beds can be easily "erased" or modified.

WHERE? Put raised beds where you want them. Ideally, they will be in areas that border high foot traffic so they create "texture" and a rolling landscape, or in places that are visible from a number of angles. Vegetable gardens need to be in full sunlight, and some flowerbeds will require more sun than others. It's important to locate your raised bed according to sunlight requirements for the types of plants that you want to grow. You might consider creating a raised bed in an area of the lawn that does not support good turf, or an area of the yard where less lawn is desirable. Any location is suitable, provided you have good reason for it, and provided sunlight conditions will accommodate the plants, flowers and vegetables you want to raise.

HOW? It always helps to have a simple plan on paper before you begin, as well as some well-thought-out ideas about the purpose of your raised bed, what you hope to accomplish with it, the types of plants you want to raise, and of course, the size and structure of your bed. Assemble all the materials you need before you start the project. You'll need some chalk line and stakes to mark the area of your new garden, enough bagged or bulk soil to fill the space, some type of support material such as timbers or rock to contain the soil, and landscape fabric for weed control, if you desire. Finally, you'll need the plants or seeds for the bed and enough mulch to cover the area.

Soil can be either bagged or bulk. Bagged soil is ideal because it contains the right amounts of organic material and other ingredients for a good growing medium. Bagged soil is easy to handle and doesn't require a lot of shoveling. Bulk soil requires a wheelbarrow and some shoveling, but might be more economical if the bed is large. Remember that soil flattens and spreads as you add it to the bed. The amount you'll need may vary, but a general rule is ten to fifteen forty-pound bags of soil for a raised bed that is ten feet long, three feet wide and twenty inches in height. Do not use inferior grade bagged soil, soil from unknown origins, or soil from existing beds that are known to have problems.

Plan according to the plants you want to grow. Annuals and perennials have shallow root systems that extend no deeper than six or eight inches. Some landscape plants, especially oleanders and gardenias, have deeper roots. Vegetable plants have short growing seasons, and crops may change several times during the year, while some perennials need to stay in the same location for several years before they are moved.

You'll need to support and brace the soil in the raised bed. Erosion can destroy the area, and you'll want to confine the bed so that specific fertilizers and growing techniques can be used right where you want them. Choose any material you like; landscape timbers are good, limestone rock is readily available, railroad ties, treated lumber, and even logs are suitable. Modern landscape fabrics, made from synthetics or jute, are quite popular for erosion control and steep grade work. These fabrics are cut to fit after applying and are attached to the ground with heavy metal staples. Trailing ground covers are then planted in holes that are cut into the fabric to contain them. The amount of support you'll need depends on the size and height of the raised bed.

After you choose the location, design the basic shape of the bed and mark it. You can treat the area with a herbicide if you choose, but it's not necessary. The remaining steps are simple. As you add soil, add support, working up to the desired level. After the entire bed is constructed, including weed control fabric, install the plants or seeds, water thoroughly, fertilize appropriately, and, finally, apply mulch as the project is completed.

❦ **DR. PLANT SAYS:** Trailing plants such as ivy and creeping thyme create interest. Put them along the sides and borders so they spill over the perimeters.

HOW TO READ A FERTILIZER LABEL

Fertilizers are sold in many forms. This information applies to bagged, granular formulas only.

WHAT? Every bag of commercially-sold fertilizer must, by law, contain a label that lists the contents.

WHO? Being able to read a fertilizer bag label gives you firsthand knowledge of the bag's contents without having to depend on others to explain it.

WHEN? Read the label carefully *before* you purchase the product.

WHY? Some fertilizers are made specifically for certain tasks, and others are used for general applications. While most fertilizers are safe for homeowner use, there are some that should be used with caution. Some fertilizers have a potential to "burn" plants and their root systems; others are so low in nutrients that they are ineffective. Knowing the values of the nutrients, their percentages, and their relation to the cost of the fertilizer can help you determine which fertilizers are best for your situation. Finally, be aware that using too much fertilizer can be dangerous. Using it improperly can be harmful to you and the environment.

WHERE? Read the label at the lawn and garden center or nursery before you purchase the product. Avoid purchasing fertilizers by mail or from catalogues.

HOW? Fertilizers contain nutrients that are necessary for plant growth. Though these nutrients are often present in ordinary garden soil, they may not be present in sufficient amounts to promote the type of growth and performance you expect. Some soils may be loaded with one or two nutrients, and greatly deficient in others.

There are three elements that are essential to plant growth: nitrogen, phosphorus, and potassium. The initials N for nitrogen, P for phosphorus, and K for potassium or potash, designate these elements. A fertilizer bag label will indicate the amount of these nutrients and is always expressed in percentages of the total contents and in the same order: nitrogen first, phosphorus second, and potash third. Therefore, the NPK shown on the label will have three numbers, separated by dashes, usually displayed on the front of the bag. An NPK of 10-10-10 contains ten percent of each of the three elements. If the bag weighs one hundred pounds, ten pounds would be nitrogen, ten pounds phosphorus, and ten pounds potash. The rest of the poundage would be rock filler or inert ingredients. When the NPK is roughly equal, the fertilizer is said to be balanced.

Some fertilizers contain less of one element and more of another. An NPK of 0-0-22 contains a lot of potash, but no nitrogen or phosphorus. An NPK of 5-10-30 contains a little nitrogen, a healthy amount of phosphorus, and a large percentage of potash.

Nitrogen is the element that gives plants their green color, vitality, and growth. Phosphorus contributes to blossom and flower development, fruit set, and root growth. Potash is essential for root system development and the plant's immune system, and contributes to water transfer through the cells. The elements work together for the overall health of the plant. One does not function without the others, though it is entirely possible for plants to benefit by adding more of one than the others. A plant that has dense, thick foliage, but few flowers, may need more P than N. A lawn in the fall of the year may need more K to help build the roots and less N to promote green-up.

In addition to the three elements, fertilizers often contain other nutrients, including sulfur, calcium, iron, zinc, molybdenum, and copper. These "trace elements" are used by plants in very small amounts, and though there is often no exact amount required, plant biologists recognize their place in plant growth and development. The best fertilizers contain these elements as a supplement to the usual NPK. These better grades of fertilizer are said to be "premium fertilizers." A fertilizer label indicating that the fertilizer is "ammoniated" means that each pellet or granule is fully charged with all the nutrients, as opposed to a blended fertilizer which contains individual pellets or granules of the different nutrients.

When there is doubt about the right fertilizer for your lawn or garden, the correct choice is usually a premium grade, low nitrogen, balanced NPK. 5-10-10 is a good example. Another wise choice is 6-6-12. In both cases, your plants will get a healthy amount of nitrogen, but not too much. They'll also receive adequate supplements of P and K to stimulate blossom development and root growth. These premium fertilizers are often ammoniated.

Of course, you can always tailor the NPK for specific purposes. 0-0-22 is an excellent choice for storm-damaged plants, weak plants, and to boost nutrition levels when no green-up or leaf growth is needed. 10-0-0 is a good choice NPK for leafy vegetables such as spinach and lettuce, or for daylilies, which benefit from extra nitrogen. 0-20-0 is the NPK for super phosphate or rock phosphate—an excellent fertilizer for bulbs or flowering plants.

Determining the right NPK for your garden should not be guesswork, but can easily be done with the help of a soil sample. Test results will often reveal exactly what your garden soil needs to promote healthy plant performance.

Choosing a fertilizer is often a matter of economics. A bag of 10-10-10 goes a lot further than a bag of 8-8-8 because the percentages of nutrients are higher. The cost difference is not significant, so you will use less of the 10-10-10 for roughly the same cost as the 8-8-8. Some specialty formulas and blends are inexpensive, yet contain percentages that are so low that several bags may be needed to accomplish the task.

Application rates vary depending on the NPK. Usually, the label will indicate a recommended rate of application for selected purposes, and the rates are usually applied to a thousand square feet. In some cases, the fertilizer label will recommend a rate for row applications, as in vegetable crops. The following guidelines might help

Michael Wolf

115

in deciding how much fertilizer you need for general purposes.
• If the N percentage is 5, use twenty pounds of fertilizer per thousand square feet.
• If the N percentage is 10, use ten pounds of fertilizer per thousand square feet.
• If the N percentage is 15, use six and a half pounds per thousand square feet.
 It is always better to dispense fertilizer with a spreader than to hand-toss it. Some fertilizers have a heavy salt content and will burn if applied too heavily in some areas. To avoid putting too much fertilizer in one spot, use a spreader.

Packaging varies, of course, but today's consumers prefer plastic forty-pound bags with accurate, detailed instructions and prominent NPKs. Some agricultural formulas are still sold in fifty-pound paper bags, but the labeling requirements are the same. Never purchase a bag without a label, and purchase whole, intact bags, not those that are torn, damaged, or incomplete.

Try to purchase fertilizers as you need them. Some bags can be opened and used partially as the season progresses, but storing fertilizer bags around the tool shed and garage is not a good idea. Purchase what you need, when you need it, and use all of it as quickly as you can.

❦ **DR. PLANT SAYS:** Some fertilizers solidify rapidly once the bag is opened. Avoid ending up with a bag of heavy, cement-like material by using your fertilizer, not storing it.

HOW TO INTERPRET
BOTANICAL NAMES AND SIGNS

WHAT? Plant labels contain brief, often coded information as well as Latin names. In many cases they are hard to read, and difficult to understand. Sometimes the information is useless, but frequently a label can help indicate the color of the bloom, as well as specific performance habits that might steer you in purchasing the plant. Usually, labels will give other information including ideal growing temperatures, exposure, and resistance to disease.

WHO? You can better understand the nature of the plant you are considering if you can read the descriptive label and its information.

WHEN? Read the label carefully while you are at the nursery or garden center, before you purchase your plant.

WHY? People purchase plants for many reasons. Some like to grow unusual, different plants that are uncommon to the area. Others prefer classic plants that are renowned for garden stability. In any case, the "tell-tag" will reveal information about your chances for success.

Botanical signs in gardens, arboretums, and nurseries are valuable tools. They not only give the name of the plant in a universal language, Latin, but they also give valuable details about the plant's history and performance.

Whether reading a sign or a tell-tag, spending time on that information may be as important as regarding the plant itself.

WHERE? Botanical signs are located front and center in most nurseries or public gardens, or in the center of a group of same-species plants. In garden centers, tell-tags are slipped into the soil in cell packs and pots, or may be attached to stems and branches in line stock. Look for the signs and tags. Sometimes they are hard to locate.

HOW? Latin is the universal plant language, and reveals a plant's "nomenclature." It gives the name of the plant in a form that will be recognized in any garden center or nursery the world over. This precision may be crucial when purchasing specific plants, as it can be confusing when many plants are given the same common name. "Sweet shrub" is a good example. Though there is a plant named sweetshrub, there are hundreds of plants in many localities called "sweet shrub" but are not the actual plant.

Purchasing a plant by its botanical name also gives you some assurance beyond a general description. There are thousands of varieties of azaleas, for example, but the one you have chosen for your landscape has a specific name. You can purchase that plant with confidence when you buy it by name, not by description, which is particularly important when you are choosing plants for growth habits and color. There are a number of shades of the color pink; to get the right shade, purchase your plant by name, not color. Some varieties of plants grow differently from others, and even though they may have the same general name, a more specific name can be used to get the plant you want for your garden.

Of course, not all plant vendors use Latin names. Some roadside nurseries, independent plant dealers, and even major garden centers find it difficult to maintain proper signage, and some don't even attempt to label plants. Try to deal with nurseries that identify their stock with proper botanical names.

Actually, labels are easy to read, and you don't have to be able to pronounce the names, just read them. The first word that denotes a group of plants with similar traits called a **genus** and is always written with a capital letter. The second word represents the more specific nature of the plant and identifies it as one of a kind. It is called the **species** of the plant. Species names are rarely capitalized. A third, more detailed identification is the cultivated variety, or **cultivar**, and is usually contained in single quotation marks. Cultivars are often

117

the result of hybridization, and when done with several species in the genus, the letter "x" will appear before the species name. When several genera are used to hybridize plants, the "x" appears before the genus. Horticultural varieties or varieties with Latin names are often written in italics. Some examples of botanical names are:

• *Prunus laurocerasus* 'Otto Luyken.' This plant is commonly known as Otto Luyken cherry laurel. *Prunus* is the genus, referring to cherries; laurocerasus is the species, referring to "laurel" type growth; and 'Otto Luyken' is the variety name given to this particular shrub.

• *Daphne x burkwoodii* 'Somerset' is the name given to a specific Burkwood hybrid daphne.

• *Spiraea x vanhouttei* is hybrid Vanhoutte's spirea.

• *x Cupressocyparis leylandii* is the famous Leyland cypress, the botanical name of which represents the hybrid cross of several genera.

Your nurseryman or plant professional can give you the specific details of a plant's performance based on its name or names. A book that lists plants may also describe them or, if you know the botanical name, you can match plants you have seen in other gardens.

Signs in public gardens are read the same way, and often will contain phonetic pronunciation tips. But it is not important to speak Latin, just important to read it.

Tell-tags are loaded with other information, most of which is self-explanatory. Planting depth, sun exposure, and ideal growing temperatures are sometimes expressed in symbols or illustrations, and flower color is sometimes actually shown. The term "F-1" hybrid simply means that the selection is a hybrid cross of the first generation, and will not produce true from seed. Another frequent designation is "PVP" followed by a patent warning, indicating that the plant is a protected variety with a pending patent and cannot be propagated by taking cuttings of the stems or leaves.

Consumers often disregard botanical signs and tell-tags. And, to be sure, some plants are labeled incorrectly. But for the most part, you'll have better results with your landscape choices and culture if you choose your plants by botanical name and follow the label instructions.

❦ **DR. PLANT SAYS:** Leave the tell-tag or descriptive tag on your new plant after you place it in your landscape. You might need to match it later, or you may want to know exactly what it is at a later date. You can also tag it with a permanent sign or enter the information in your garden notebook. There is no difference between your garden and a public garden in this regard.

HOW TO TAKE A SOIL SAMPLE

WHAT? Soil testing by a competent lab is the only way to determine the nature of your soil and its pH. There are some reliable home test kits, but taking a sample and sending it to a lab for analysis is the best method. The results are complete and detailed, and offer specific steps to change or modify your soil and its pH.

WHO? You should take your own soil samples, or you can supervise the task.

WHEN? Soil samples need to be dry and warm; warm soil tests better because when the soil is above sixty degrees more elements are present in the top twelve inches of the soil. The best time of the year is mid-spring, but fall testing is frequently done. It can take up to several weeks to get the results, especially if the labs are busy. One test each year is sufficient unless you are growing a commercial crop. The results of your test may advise you to modify your soil with lime, which could take several months to take effect. Plan sampling dates accordingly. Many gardeners test their soil in the summer, especially if they have problems.

WHY? Knowing the nature of your soil determines the types of fertilizers you'll need, if you need to change the structure of your soil, and if you need to change the pH. Plants trying to grow in unsuitable conditions may never perform well, and could eventually fail. You can avoid expensive repair by modifying your soil, and knowing the nature of your soil can make the difference between a landscape that thrives and one that merely survives. All the fertilizer in the world will not help plants that are growing in heavy soils, wet soils, or soils that have the wrong pH. The only way to gain that information is to test. Testing begins with a good sample.

WHERE? Select several sites for sampling. Choose areas of the lawn that are performing below standard, or divide the lawn into sections, such as the front and back. Test your main flowerbeds, the vegetable garden, and specific sites such as annual color gardens, perennial gardens, and raised beds.

HOW? Assemble all the tools and materials before you start. You'll need some quart-size plastic bags, a permanent marker, a bucket, and a trowel. Boxes for soil samples are available at the Cooperative Extension office closest to you. You can pick them up before you sample, or take your samples to their office in bags, but their boxes have to be used to ship the samples to the lab.

Select a site—the front lawn, for example—and label a bag or box accordingly. Take a sample of the soil by digging to a depth of six or eight inches, pulling some soil from the bottom, some soil mid-way, and some from the surface. Mix the three samples in the bucket and pour the mixture into the bag or box. Make sure the container is labeled. Repeat the same process in each location.

If you take your samples to the Extension office in bags, do so quickly. Don't let the soil stand in the bag for any length of time before transferring it to an official sample box. There are microbes in the soil (both good and bad) that will show up if the testing is done quickly. Some offices charge for soil testing, but the fee is nominal.

When you receive the test results, they will be detailed and extensive and will contain much information that you might not understand. There will usually be a letter with an explanation guide and a key to interpreting the analysis. Each test site will have a different report, so it is important to keep a record of your test sites and how you labeled them.

Pay close attention to the pH reading and the recommendations for fertilizing. These recommendations are based on the structure of the sample, its actual pH, and its deficiencies in basic nutrients. The test lab may also suggest adding organic matter, sand, or clay to your soil as conditioners.

❦ **DR. PLANT SAYS:** Expensive pH meters that measure soil acidity with a probe are not as reliable as proper testing. Test kits that require mixing chemicals, water, and soil, and then pouring solutions into different vials are often confusing and difficult to use. For simplicity and ease in understanding, there is no test like the official Department of Agriculture test. It is worth the effort and wait.

HOW TO TEST FOR SOIL COMPACTION

WHAT? Typical soils in the coastal area of the South are sandy and well-drained. But some homesites and developed areas are built on filled land that historically is wet and more compacted. In many cases, fill material consists of heavy soil that does not drain well. If your garden or flowerbed retains too much water and does not drain well, you'll never have flowers and plants that thrive. Testing for basic soil compaction is essential if you suspect a drainage problem.

WHO? This is an easy test that you can do without much difficulty.

WHEN? Spring is the best time of year for this test—after the soil is warm, but not during a rainy spell.

WHY? Test the compaction of your garden so you can modify its structure.

WHERE? Any section of the lawn or garden where you suspect that the soil is compacted. Water may stand for long periods of time, or may run off without soaking the soil. In either case, test it if you are suspicious.

HOW? In the suspect area, dig a hole the size of an upended shoebox—about ten inches deep and six inches square. Fill it with water and allow it to drain completely. Refill the same hole with water a second time and allow it to drain, this time keeping track of how long it takes to empty. If the hole does not drain completely in six hours, the soil in the area is too compacted and will need modifying.

You can modify soil with several types of materials to enhance drainage. Vermiculite is often used. Perlite is also a good choice. Sharp sand or builder's sand is the traditional material, and there are several new ceramic products that are now being used on golf course greens to displace water.

HOW TO COMPOST

WHAT? Composting was once a routine performed by organic gardeners and few others. Today it is part of everyday life for many people: those who choose to compost for environmental reasons, and those who use compost in commercial growing operations. The value of compost, often called "black gold," is well established and should be a basic part of your gardening style. It is used to supplement flowerbeds and vegetable gardens, to apply over dormant lawns, and to generate the best growing medium for potted plants and hanging baskets. Essentially decomposed organic matter, compost is rich in nutrients, vital plant trace elements, beneficial microbes, and soil enhancers. It neutralizes soil pH and improves the structure of ordinary garden soil.

Michael Wolf • Taken at the New Hanover County Cooperative Extension

WHO? You can do this easy project yourself, hire a carpenter to make a compost bin, or purchase a mechanical compost maker. There are some county and municipal agencies that supply homeowners with free compost bins that are made from recycled pallets.

WHEN? Composting is a year-round event.

WHY? Not only does compost provide a ready source of rich garden organic matter, it is essential for optimum plant growth and development. It recycles garden and kitchen waste, relieves the pressure on landfills, and can reduce the amount of fertilizers you use. It is an economical way to build soil, and offers a source of excellent garden soil.

WHERE? Compost bins, piles, or heaps should be located in an out-of-the-way section of the garden, but in an area that gets a considerable amount of sunlight and is close to a water supply. Some gardeners feature their compost bins as decorative items that fit naturally into their landscape plan.

HOW? Numerous books have been written on the subject of composting. Some people get very technical and serious about the subject, while others simply "do a little composting." The extent of your composting experience depends on your lifestyle and gardening habits, but the important thing is to compost organic scraps at some level. You will be richly rewarded in any case.

Passive composting is the simplest form: enclose an area with braces, welded wire, chicken wire or anything that will contain vegetable matter, and use this place to discard vegetable matter. Passive composting does not generate heat.

Active composting is structured and requires more attention. You'll need to build or purchase a compost bin. The essentials are an enclosure with three sides and a "door," a solid floor (which can be the ground), and easy access for turning and rotating the ingredients. The container for an active compost pile needs to build and retain heat—one of the key ingredients in active composting.

If you want to build compost in a passive heap, start with a bag or two of potting soil in the enclosure, and add any organic vegetable scraps from the kitchen. Coffee grounds, eggshells, plant trimmings, lawn clippings, and vegetable matter from the garden are also good for composting. Do not use animal matter, foods with oils or fats, weeds, diseased plants, or sticks and branches larger than a pencil. Use a spade or shovel to turn or stir the heap from time to time, and make sure it stays moist, but not wet. Over time, the passive pile will decompose, and the result will be a rich, organic material perfectly suited for plant growth, especially when combined with ordinary potting soil or garden soil.

Active composting requires three main ingredients: a source of nitrogen to help generate heat, water to help decompose matter, and fuel, which consists of the garden and kitchen refuse you'll be adding to the pile. Begin the process by stocking the enclosure with some potting soil, bagged soil or excellent garden soil, and a healthy amount of humus. Stir in some organic nitrogen, such as cottonseed meal or soy meal. Most lawn and garden centers now sell "compost makers" which are organic sources of nitrogen combined with microbes to initiate composting activity when combined with fuel and water.

You can add garden material, leaves, grass clippings, kitchen scraps, small trimmings from shrubs, and just about any vegetable matter that would usually get tossed into the garbage. The enclosure must be tight enough to generate and retain the heat that will build as you add material, and you must be able to stir and rotate the pile from top to bottom. Each time you add fuel, add some water and stir the pile. Generating compost in an active pile takes several weeks, but after the initial start-up process, you'll have ready-to-use compost, provided you follow the procedure and add fuel regularly.

There are some important guidelines to follow when composting. Although active piles generate substantial heat, the heat is not high enough to kill some weed seeds; therefore, weeds should be destroyed, not composted. Some plant pathogens, including damping off disease and tomato wilt disease, are not destroyed in ordinary composting. Thus, annuals that die from disease, tomatoes that are killed by wilt, and plant trimmings that have fungal disorders should not go into the compost heap. Keep animal products out of the compost bin; commercial fertilizers have no place in organic compost; and serious gardeners don't like to add synthetic material to compost. Plants treated with pesticides, especially weed killers, don't belong in the compost heap.

You may need to add some soil from time to time. If you do so, you should use the best grade potting soil possible, or soil from a reliable, safe source. Be sure to use your compost. There is no point in storing it.

Most Cooperative Extension Service offices have compost demonstration sites, and many have classes, seminars, and bulletins on how to compost. There are many additional sources for information on how to create the best compost: books, magazines, articles, and the Internet. The methods and materials may vary, but the important thing is to compost on your own level and do it as a basic part of your lawn and garden hobby.

❧ **DR. PLANT SAYS:** A quick and easy way to generate compost is to fill a plastic trash bag with leaves or lawn clippings, add a shovel full of good quality soil and a shovel full of 8-8-8 or 10-10-10 fertilizer. Seal the bag and store it in a sunny spot for a few months. You'll have some excellent compost for use in the garden.

☙ **DR. PLANT SAYS:** Wood ashes are not the same as ashes from the charcoal grill. You can add some wood ashes to your compost from your hardwood fire; these ashes are rich in nutrients and will sweeten soil by making it less acid. Not all charcoal comes from hardwood, and ashes from charcoal fires contain a number of elements that are not suitable for compost piles.

THE LAWN AND GARDEN MEDICINE CHEST AND TOOL BOX

WHAT? A toolbox or satchel that contains some basic tools and materials, readily accessible and easy to carry, can be a handy and much-used part of your basic garden tool inventory.

WHO? Anyone who gardens as a hobby should have a garden medicine chest and a tool-box on hand for quick, ordinary chores.

WHEN? If you are serious about gardening as a hobby, put this project first on the list. Check your toolbox regularly, keeping it up-to-date.

WHY? As you will see in the list of tools and remedies, some items will be used constantly, while others might be used once in a while. When visiting plant swaps or friends' gardens, you might see a plant that you'd like to propagate; in such instances, you would use specific items that might be very different from your everyday tools. Small tools and quick-fixes are more quickly accessed from a basic toolbox, rather than from the shelves of the shed or garage.

WHERE? Keep your toolbox and medicine chest handy. Some serious gardeners even keep it in the trunk of the car.

HOW? How do you know what to include in your toolbox or medicine chest? The contents will vary depending on your method of gardening, but you'll find these items are used frequently in curing problems, collecting plants, gathering seeds, and healing wounds.

Use a sturdy, waterproof box that has a good handle and has enough room for the following: a folding knife with a sharp blade, standard by-pass garden shears, a hand trowel, a claw hammer, scissors, latex gloves, garden gloves, and a ball of twine. For plant propagation, the box should have a small bag of vermiculite, several eight ounce-plastic cups, a small bag of sphagnum moss, some aluminum foil, a bottle of Rootone, a pair of tweezers, and a roll of duct tape.

For pest control, pack a box of baking soda, a small bottle of pre-mixed pyrethrin insecticide, a small bag of Rotenone dust, a small bag of Dipel worm killer, a bottle of antiseptic mouthwash, a bottle of water, and some liquid soap.

For general garden use, seed gathering, and sampling, have some plastic bags with twist ties. And for personal use, include some insect repellent, a tube of cortisone cream or calamine lotion, a small pad for writing notes, a pencil, and a small first-aid kit.

You may not need some of the supplies at all; others you may use frequently. Of course, you can add or discard items depending on your gardening style.

❦ DR. PLANT SAYS: The most valuable tool in your box is your knife.

HOW TO MOW THE LAWN

WHAT? There are some techniques for lawn care and mowing that will add life to the grass and create a healthy, attractive appearance.

WHO? You can mow your own lawn, or make sure your lawn and garden professional knows your method of lawn care.

WHEN? You can follow these tips and methods whenever you cut the grass. It is always best to stay with a definite program through the lawn season, following the same procedures every time you mow.

WHY? Most homeowners approach lawn care and mowing as an onerous, necessary task. In addition to maintaining a basic appearance, mowing is also a vital part of the health of the lawn. When done properly, it can extend the life of a lawn, build pest resistance, and create a one-of-a-kind appearance that marks your turf as distinctive. It's not an art form, of course, but creating an interesting lawn can be an enjoyable experience. Mowing can be a part of an overall plan for an attractive turf, not just the end result of water and fertilizer.

WHERE? Consider this method for all parts of your lawn, not just those sections that are visible from the street or have high foot traffic.

HOW? Choosing the right equipment is essential. Gasoline-powered rotary mowers are standard issue these days, but there are also powered reel-type mowers that give a razored, manicured look, as well as electric mowers powered with extension cords. Manual reel mow-

Michael Wolf

ers, the kind that kids in the '50s used for Saturday grass cutting, are still around and are sur-prisingly popular among environmentally-concerned people who like less noise pollution and good old-fashioned exercise.

Most warm-season turf responds better to gasoline rotary mowers than to other types of machines. Bermuda and zoysia lawns need a reel mower to cut them correctly but, for the most part, summer turf in the coastal South usually gets cut with rotary mowers. There are a number of makes and models, of course, but push mowers are the ones most frequently sold. There are some powered push mowers that have extra drives and belts that propel the wheels, making them "self-propelled" models, but you still have to walk behind them and push them along. If you mow your grass on a regular basis, and don't allow it to get tough and coarse, you'll do just fine without a self-propelled model.

Some mowers have wider decks than others, offering longer mower blades. Consider the cost of the machine in relation to the width of the deck. If a thirty-inch cut will reduce the number of trips up and down the lawn, thus saving time, then a wide deck is a good choice. But if a twenty six-inch cut will do just as well for less money, and if the time saved is not sig-nificant, you are wise to avoid spending the extra money.

The popular mulching mowers are designed to eliminate the need to rake and collect grass cuttings. There are many mowers that have side discharge or rear bag collection, but stopping to empty bags, raking the lawn after cutting, and then disposing of lawn clippings in plastic bags curbside are things of the past. Time and energy, environmental concerns, and convenience dictate mulching decks, especially when such a vital resource as grass clippings can be added directly back to the turf.

In addition to these basic considerations, your mower will give you many seasons of performance if you mow the lawn properly, make sure the blades are sharp each time you cut the lawn, and keep your machine in tip-top shape. (See the section on lawn mower maintenance.)

Mow the lawn when the grass is dry and clear of debris. Mornings may be suitable, but anytime is a good time to cut the grass, provided you don't get overheated on a summer day, and the neighborhood won't be irritated by noise from your mower. Walk your lawn first to make sure pine cones, branches, sticks, and rocks won't chip the mower blade. Check for dog droppings and obstacles that will interfere with your project. To save some time while mowing, clumps of coarse grass can be whittled down with your line trimmer before you start.

Cut the grass in straight lines, saving curves and angles for trimming at the end of the job. Never cut over the same swath twice, and try to cut as long a line as possible without breaking stride. Develop several patterns of lines, and use a different pattern each time you mow. For example, mow the lawn in length strips one week and in width strips the following week. Try to avoid backing up and re-cutting the same section. Stay focused on the job, be sensible about breaks and breathers, but allow enough time to complete the job at hand so you'll avoid having an incomplete mowing job.

Use your mower or line trimmer to finish curves and angles, choosing the right machine for the task. If you find yourself pushing and pulling the mower back and forth under hedges and shrubbery, you may be using the wrong tool. **(Caution!! Be careful with your line trimmer around sensitive plants. "Girdling" trunks of some shrubs will kill plants, and many fine seedlings have been needlessly killed by errant line trimmers.)**

To avoid scalping the lawn, smooth ridges and eliminate depressions before the season gets underway. If you mow along ditch banks and inclines, walk up and down the rise, not the length of the bank. Any grade steeper than forty-five degrees poses a safety risk; the mower can easily flip backwards or get away from you if the grade is too steep for comfortable walking with the machine. Rather than planting turf in these areas, you might consider a ground cover that does not require mowing.

Many landscapers install "mowing strips." These eight- or ten-inch wide strips around the perimeters of the lawn are mulch-covered, brick, or hard-surfaced areas that allow for mower turn-around and can be cleaned with organic herbicides or line trimmers, not lawn mowers.

As with any power tool, safety is the most important factor. Wear steel-toe safety boots, eye protection, and noise eliminators. Some lawn care specialists recommend wearing old-fashioned golf shoes with spikes so the turf will be aerated as you walk.

HOW TO STORE YOUR LAWN MOWER FOR THE WINTER, ANDHOW TO PERFORM SOME BASIC LAWN MOWER MAINTENANCE

(Note: See the section on disposal of combustibles, household chemicals and lawn and garden chemicals.)

WHAT? These basic steps in lawn mower maintenance not only prepare your mower for winter storage, but also keep your mower in good running order for the lawn grass season.

WHO? This is a task that you can do yourself, or you can take the mower to a certified professional small engine mechanic.

WHEN? As soon as your lawn is dormant for the winter (probably towards the end of November), and you have cut the grass for the final time, store your mower until the spring. If, on the other hand, you decide to do simple servicing, once a month is normal procedure.

WHY? Many lawn problems start with faulty equipment. Lopsided mower blades that wobble the mower deck and create off-balance cuts, improper deck settings that scalp the lawn or cut it too closely, poor engine performance that strains the mower and creates pollution, or general ill repair that creates strain and extra work for the gardener are all typical. Maintaining the landscape should be enjoyable, but nothing is more frustrating than equipment that won't start or runs improperly, and jobs that have to be interrupted because the mower malfunctions. These irritating situations can be controlled, if not eliminated altogether with some simple maintenance.

WHERE? You'll need a workbench in your garage or tool room so this job can be done on a rainy day. Good lighting is necessary and quick access to tools is helpful. Obviously, you'll need plenty of space in which to work.

HOW? There are six things to do when storing the mower or doing monthly maintenance. Go step-by-step with a checklist. Assemble all your parts and tools before you start. Keep accurate records and notes. *Safety first!* Remember to protect the environment and those around you while you are working.

BEFORE YOU BEGIN WORK, DISCONNECT THE SPARK PLUG!

1. You'll need to make sure that all gas is out of the mower before you store it. You can run the mower until the gas is used up, or you can use an approved container to take the gas to a recycling facility. Be careful, and wipe up any spills, although you can avoid spill problems by working on some sheets of newspaper. Don't do this job on bare sections of lawn grass.

   If you are doing monthly maintenance, you won't need to drain the tank, simply check the fuel level and general appearance of the mower.

DON'T DISPOSE OF GASOLINE BY POURING IT INTO THE GROUND. YOUR CONTAINER CAN BE DISCARDED AT SITES THAT HANDLE COMBUSTIBLES, OR AT A LOCATION RECOMMENDED BY THE COOPERATIVE EXTENSION SERVICE. DISPOSE OF YOUR CONTAINER QUICKLY. DON'T ALLOW OLD FUEL TO STAY AROUND THE HOUSE OR GARAGE.

   Many lawn mowers have an in-line fuel filter. You won't need to replace it if you are doing your monthly maintenance; simply check it to make sure it is clean and clear. If you are storing the mower for the winter, replace the fuel filter with a new one.

2. Change the engine oil. Some lawn mowers have an oil drain plug that makes draining the engine oil easy. Most do not, so you'll have to tip the mower or tilt it so the oil drains through the oil fill plug on the side of the engine. This is the same port that contains the dipstick. Remove the cap, tilt the mower and drain the oil into a suitable container. You can take the oil to a recycling center, or to one of several gas stations or auto supply stores that accept used oil for recycling. If you are storing the mower, or doing routine maintenance, be sure to refill the engine block with the correct amount of recommended small engine motor oil. Use a funnel to fill the engine, avoiding spills.

3. Change the mower blade. While the gas tank is empty, tilt the mower back (not on its side) to expose the blade. Secure the mower so it won't roll or slide backward and, using the right size wrench, remove the bolt that attaches the blade to the mower. If you have trouble removing the bolt, try some bolt-loosening spray, a basic spray lubricant, or a socket wrench with a larger handle for more torque. Wear gloves so you won't skin your knuckles.

   Once the blade is removed, clean the underside of the deck. Replace the old blade with a new blade from your hardware store or small-engine supply house. Although you can attempt sharpening the old blade with a file, you probably will never get the correct balance and loft on the old blade. Balance and loft are important so that the blade "picks up" the grass and cuts it correctly. If the blade is not sharpened correctly, it will not spin correctly and the lawn will show the effect.

Regardless of the tools you have, you'll probably never attain the original balance and sharpness of the blade. Unless you get a professional to sharpen it for you, simply replace the old blade with a new one. Nothing beats a new, sharp, balanced mower blade for accurate lawn mowing. Be sure to take the old blade to the supply house with you to avoid getting the wrong part. You might also consider leaving the old blade for professional sharpening; you can always use it later as an emergency blade.

4. Return the mower to its normal position and remove the spark plug. You'll need a spark plug wrench, which is readily available at your hardware store or small engine parts house. Be sure to take the old plug to the parts house so you can get the proper match; don't rely on your memory. Replace the old plug with the new one, making sure that the gap is correct according to the manufacturer's specifications. Under normal conditions, a spark plug will last a season—so you won't have to replace it every month during the summer, but you should remove it and clean it. If you are storing your mower for the winter, replace the plug.

5. The air filter on most mowers is easy to locate and change. You'll need a screwdriver to remove the filter from the housing. You can replace the foam pad filter or clean the old one with soapy water (avoid cleaning the air filter with solvent). This task is crucial to good engine maintenance and winter storage, as a dirty air filter can lead to major engine problems.

6. Before reconnecting the spark plug, clean the top of the mower deck and the chutes. Oil the cables and connections, paying close attention to the choke and throttle arm.

Remember! These are simple tasks that you can do at home, but if you have any doubts, take your mower to a professional repairman. Careless mistakes can result in serious injury to you, the mower, and the lawn and garden!

Finally, check all your work. Are bolts tightened and secure? Oil or gasoline spills removed? Connections in order? If your job is complete, be sure to make the proper notes in your maintenance journal or garden notebook.

HOMEMADE ORGANIC ALTERNATIVES TO SYNTHETIC PESTICIDES

WHAT? Next to fertilizers, pesticides lead sales in most garden centers. There are hundreds of insect killers, weed killers, and disease controls from which to choose, and the options can be confusing. Recognizing the trend towards gardening simplicity, many pesticide makers have developed "one-size-fits-all" treatments designed to solve a number of problems with one spray or dust. Some of these convenient treatments are organic in nature and are environmentally friendly. Others are synthetic and may be more invasive. But the standard treatment for most problems is still the specific application of a chemical pesticide designed to eliminate that problem. The problem can be common and simple, such as aphids, or rare and complex, like the fungal disease that has destroyed so many of our Red Tips.

WHO? You are solely responsible for the care of your landscape. Your choices for pesticides (insecticides, fungicides, and herbicides) can be organic or synthetic, depending on your situation. Most states require persons who apply pesticides to property other than their own to have licenses and permits. If you allow someone to treat your landscape with a chemical application, be sure he is properly licensed and insured. But whether you hire someone to do it for you, or you do it yourself, you are ultimately responsible for the care and maintenance of your lawn and garden.

WHEN? You should treat problems in the landscape with caution. First, decide if you really have a problem that will require a pesticide. (There is a section in this book that will help you do just that.) Be sure that treatment is necessary before you spray or dust. Once you've determined that you have a problem that needs treating, do it quickly, safely, and efficiently. Whether you use an organic homemade treatment or a synthetic one, the time to apply it depends on the severity of the case. Once you have decided, proceed as quickly as possible.

WHY? Of course you could simply allow pests to control the garden. Many gardeners do just that. Afraid of using any pesticides, they sacrifice beautiful landscapes to weeds, disease, and insects.

The way to maintain your landscape is to control those things that destroy its beauty, and to eliminate the things that make a joke of your hard efforts. You would be foolish to waste time and money on a garden that you are willing to give up to disease.

That said, keep in mind that you'd be equally foolish to indiscriminately destroy plants and animals that contribute to the balance of a healthy and beautiful garden. Careful use of pesticides and consideration for the environment are imperative for responsible gardening in today's society. Clearly, when offered a choice of less invasive techniques over harsher synthetic applications, the decision is elementary. On the other hand, problem-solving requires quick action and thorough treatment with a product best suited to the task.

WHERE? Decide on treatments *before* you go to the lawn and garden center. If you decide to use a synthetic application, it's best to decide what you need while looking at your garden.

HOW? Following are several homemade, organic alternatives to some of the popular synthetic pesticides used in everyday gardening. Use the one you feel is best suited for the problem you face, and never combine treatments or mix them with fertilizers.

1. This basic herbicide is designed to kill weeds or any foliage—not only contact, but through the roots as well. It will kill anything it touches, so it cannot be applied to lawn grass, ornamental flowerbeds or in the root zones of most garden plants. It is good for weed control in the driveway, walkway, or ditch bank, and can be applied to surface weeds in mulched areas.

All-Purpose Herbicide
1 quart white vinegar
1 cup table salt
1/4 cup laundry detergent

Add enough water to make one gallon. Use as needed through a household sprayer or pour directly onto plants.

2. The following insecticide is very effective and will kill nearly any insect, but is very toxic to honeybees and should be used with caution. You can keep it in the refrigerator for up to two weeks. No insect has ever developed a resistance to this nicotine-based spray.

Nicotine Insecticide
Steep one pack of loose leaf chewing tobacco or non-filtered cigarettes in 2 quarts of warm water for two hours. Strain through a cheesecloth, and add the following:

1 Tbs. household ammonia
1 Tbs. dish detergent

> 1 Tbs. baking soda
> 1 tsp. rubbing alcohol
> Enough water to make one gallon of liquid.

Use with caution, and avoid letting the spray drift.

3.   The following basic garden insecticide can be used for nearly all applications, and can be applied every eight days as needed to gain control of any insect. It works quite well for houseplants, and can be applied indoors.

> **Basic Insecticide**
> 1 Tbs. flea and tick pet shampoo
> 1 Tbs. baking soda
> 1 Tbs. household ammonia
> 1 tsp. rubbing alcohol
> Enough water to make one gallon of liquid.

 Dispense through a household sprayer with a forceful stream. Try to hit as many insects as possible.

4.   You can use this basic fungicide for all-purpose disease control and the prevention of fungal diseases in ornamentals and vegetable gardens.

> **Basic Fungicide**
> 1 Tbs. dishwashing detergent
> 2 Tbs. baking soda
> 3 quarts of water

Spray this mixture on mature foliage. Applying to healthy leaves and plant parts will often prevent the spread of disease, but applying it to plant parts that are already affected may not cure them. This organic fungicide is particularly effective in the vegetable garden.

❦ **DR. PLANT SAYS:** There are some modern insect controls that use sticky traps and lures. These traps are environmentally safe for most beneficial insects because they use specific sex lures for targeted insects. Consider using your hand-held vacuum as much as possible. You'll be surprised at the number of insects it will collect!

THE HURRICANE PREPARATION CHECK LIST

WHAT? This is a basic hurricane preparation checklist that can be posted or simply followed before the storm season starts in June.

WHO? You should do this to make sure it is done to your satisfaction.

WHEN? As with anything else related to hurricanes, take care of this task in the early summer so you'll be prepared. Don't wait until it's too late!

WHY? The reasons for these chores are obvious; the more prepared you are, the better chance you'll have of surviving a bad storm with minor damage.

WHERE? All areas of your landscape should be considered, even those that border or overlap your neighbor's property. Rather than debating whose obligation it is to remove trees from fence lines and utility lines, assume some reasonable care for your property as well as that of others and do the right thing. Remember, it doesn't matter whose tree is down on the power lines; the power is still off.

HOW? Here is the basic checklist for normal pre-season attention: Make sure overhanging limbs are removed above utility lines. **(Call the utility company or your arborist...don't do this yourself!)**

1. Remove dead, diseased, or damaged limbs and trees from the landscape; prune tree limbs that are close to or overhang the house; straighten or remove trees that are leaning more than forty-five degrees; raise or place in raised beds valuable plants and flowerbeds that are prone to flooding.

2. Eliminate weeds from ditches and ditch banks; clear obstructions from storm drains and lines; and notify the highway department of right-of-ways that are unkempt.

3. Remove piles of debris, leaf piles, and excess piles of rubbish.

4. Get rid of partially-used bags of fertilizer and pesticides.

5. Keep garden hoses coiled and out of the garden and lawn area.

6. Clear the floor of the shed or tool area that may be prone to flooding or high water.

7. Keep your garden tools in excellent repair.

8. Make sure window boxes and wall hangers are secure and firmly attached to the house.

9. Keep foundation plants pruned below window height, and hedges sheared to proper levels.

10. Make sure mulch is high and dry, and keep the landscape groomed.

11. Eliminate fire ants, hornet nests and yellow jacket hives, and clear areas in the landscape that might harbor rodents.

12. Firmly secure landscape timbers, borders and braces that are made of wood, and above-ground wood structures like compost bins, to avoid floating or damage from high winds.

13. Survey the landscape every month during the season so you can spot potential problems and eliminate them quickly.

In the event of an impending storm, there are some chores that will prevent serious damage.

1. Secure all potted plants by bringing them indoors or placing them in a secure, wind-proof area.

2. Put larger plants on their sides to prevent blowing and excessive wind damage.

3. Clear the floors of tool rooms and garden sheds that may flood.

4. Place power tools and lawnmowers on raised shelves or off the floor to prevent damage from flooding; secure garden trailers in the same manner as boats—either with weights or by turning them over to prevent storm damage; and stack bags of mulch or compost in high and dry places.

5. Clear the deck and patio of hanging baskets, umbrellas, wind chimes, grills, and bird feeders.

6. Make sure your firewood is stacked and secure.

7. Secure loose buckets, watering cans, and garden accessories that might blow away.

You'll need some gasoline and oil for your chainsaw and other power tools when the storm is over, a few extra large tarps, quick access to hand tools, rakes, and brooms. Make sure you have adequate insect repellent.

Hummingbirds and wild birds will need plenty of food after the storm passes, so keep some food handy and make sure you have ready access to bird feeders so you can get them up as soon as the storm is over.

❧ **DR. PLANT SAYS:** English ivy is susceptible to bacterial wilt if the foliage stands in water for any length of time. Ivy baskets and potted plants should be stored for the storm, but not placed on the ground where they get soaked. Bring them inside if possible. Ivy wilt kills a plant quickly, and there is no cure.

POST-HURRICANE REPAIR

WHAT? Besides the obvious, there are some things you'll need to do following a storm to make sure your landscape survives.

WHO? You can do this yourself, given time, or hire some extra help if needed. Heavy lifting can strain muscles, taking you out of the clean-up altogether. Don't attempt major tree work without a tree surgeon.

WHEN? As soon as practical after the hurricane passes, survey the landscape to determine the extent of the damage. Don't just attack the clean-up project; some jobs may take precedence, so survey before you start and develop a sensible plan of action.

WHY? We all know people who don't clean up after any storm, even a hurricane. If for no other reason than for appearance's sake, get your clean-up done as soon as possible.

WHERE? After your survey, start with the most important jobs first, keeping in mind that working with a neighbor in his yard may help restore utilities faster, help emergency vehicles gain access to the neighborhood, or allow neighbors to return home on cleared roadways.

When focusing on your personal property, your first concern will surely be your home, then the landscape. When it's time to work on the lawn and garden, tackle the hardest-hit areas first.

HOW? Be sure to take some pictures of all damage, including what was done to the lawn and garden. Insurance companies need documentation, and you'll want a visible record of what happened.

1. Locate the place in your garden where debris will be stacked. Municipal governments usually collect yard debris, but they need good access. Put the debris pile in a place where a front-end loader and dump truck can reach the debris and collect it without further damaging the landscape. Keep the site away from the mailbox and utility poles.

2. Safety first! Wear proper clothing, insect repellent, and gloves. Steel toe shoes or boots are essential, as are eye and ear protectors.

3. Hurricane debris should always be piled. Not only do many communities ban burning, but the environmental damage done by burning is extensive.

4. Heavy-duty jobs go first. Major limb removal and downed trees need to be cleared so lanes and paths can be opened for raking and general clean-up. Haul what you can; larger material can be sawed or axed. Start in the vicinity of the debris pile first, working in a circle to open more cleared areas.

5. Use your tarps for stacking and dragging material to the pile.

6. When the landscape has been cleared of as much debris as possible, you can begin to repair individual plants. Weather permitting, restore hanging baskets and potted plants, garden accessories, and outdoor furniture. The faster you re-establish familiar objects, the faster you'll get a feeling of recovery.

7. Plants that are leaning can be righted quickly while the soil is wet and the root systems are still pliable. Waste no time getting them upright again, making the entire move in one step, and stake or support them as necessary. To eliminate abrasion, use old nylon stockings for plant ties or ropes that are threaded through sections of garden hose. A three-way staking system is always best, attaching lines to three stakes and to the shrub, but any support at this point in the recovery is better than none at all. Allowing the plant to fall or lean repeatedly is harmful.

You can right trees the same way. Any tree that is leaning a few "poles" to one side (a "pole" is the width of a utility pole) can be easily righted with ropes and supports. Often it will go right back to its original position without supports. Use whatever tools you have at hand to get the job done. Come-alongs are excellent tools to right larger shrubs and small trees, but you can even use your car to push or pull trees back into position. Work quickly in the soft soil so damage will be lessened.

8. Check around the root systems of trees and shrubs. If you see exposed roots or washouts, press some compost mixed with sharp sand into the depressions to eliminate air pockets and sink holes around plants' roots.

9. Salt-water damage is not a great threat because salt water drains quickly through the soil to a level below the roots of most plants. To be on the safe side, you can apply six pounds of landplaster or calcium carbonate per hundred square feet of lawn or garden space to help control damage from salt overwash. Fresh-water flushing is the best cure for salt-water damage.

10. Do not prune any plants, except those that have damaged parts. The high winds may have desiccated branches and stripped them of foliage, but they will most likely recover. If you prune them, you'll eliminate bloom potential in some plants, and cause shrubbery to repair yet another section of the plant that is undergoing stress. Later in the year, you'll have adequate time to prune if necessary.

11. Avoid fertilizers. Strong nitrogen fertilizers are the last things you need to add to the landscape, especially in environmentally sensitive areas that are subject to severe storm water runoff. Stressed plants simply don't need growth stimulants. Three or four weeks after the storm, you can apply a light application of 0-0-22, which is rich in potash, the root system builder, and contains trace elements that may have been leached by heavy rains.

12. If your lawn or garden was subjected to standing water, you'll be encountering the effects for several months after the storm. Sensitive plants, including camellias and ligustrums, or plants with deep root systems, will probably suffer long after general storm damage has been cleared. Keep a watchful eye. Plants that fail a month or more after the storm may do so because of standing water. They will have to be removed.

13. You can safely repair split branches and broken limbs with stainless steel nuts, bolts, and washers. Drill one or more holes through damaged branches and bolt them into place. You'll need some help holding pieces together to make sure you get a secure and snug fit. Don't tie branches together with rope, twine, or wire; the resulting restrictions placed on the outside bark will inhibit the flow of water and nutrients though the stems and branches.

14. Be sure to keep accurate records and notes of events so you can plan for the next storm season.

HOW TO APPLY INSECTICIDES AND FUNGICIDES

WHAT? From time to time you will need a chemical application in your lawn and garden to correct pathogenic problems. There are some considerations, mostly regarding safety, but there are also recommendations for the best way to accomplish the task.

WHO? You can do this yourself, or you can hire a licensed chemical applicator to do the job for you.

WHEN? Any time you apply a chemical to your landscape you run some risks, either to the environment or to yourself. The risks apply to organic chemicals as well as synthetics. Whenever you treat problems with chemicals, you should always be careful to follow the step-by-step method described in the following section.

WHY? If you have anything other than a passing interest in the lawn and garden, it is particularly foolish not to solve pathogenic problems. Valuable plants need protection. Your investment in the landscape needs protection. The difference between a healthy landscape and one that greets you with ill health and poor appearances can make the difference in your daily attitude. There is no point in dealing with a sick lawn or garden when the cure may be quite simple, economical and safe.

WHERE? Apply chemicals to **your landscape only**, and make sure you have a specific target, not just a general range. It is the height of irresponsibility to allow your chemical applications to drift onto other people's properties, or to use a chemical in a manner inconsistent with the label.

HOW? There are several steps to follow in treating the landscape with a chemical. For best results, follow them accurately.

1. Identify or determine if there is a problem. A few damaged leaves or a bug or two doesn't require treatment. Your first strategy should be to do nothing. Nature may take care of it; beneficial insects control harmful insects, and weather, birds or the environment in general may solve the matter for you.

2. Diagnose the problem correctly. (See page # 143 for the section on troubleshooting.) Before you purchase a chemical application, make sure you have chosen wisely. Fungicides control diseases. Insecticides control insects. Sometimes you'll need both, but you'll need to know with some degree of certainty what chemical is best for your situation.

As a general rule, the Cooperative Extension Service in your county will have a plant pathology service available to you that will diagnose problems. Often, the Master Gardeners Association will offer a garden hotline and plant clinic as well. Get a second opinion of your diagnosis, and use the trained professionals in your area as your main source of garden information.

3. To avoid confusion when you get there, decide on your choice of applications before you go to the lawn and garden center. No one knows your lawn and garden better than you do, and the more sure you are of the problem and how to solve it, the better the results. If you need help, take a sample of the problem to show the trained people at the store.

4. Choose your weapon. Hose-end sprayers are easy to operate, but can be confusing about application and discharge rates. Pressure tank sprayers are much more reliable, but require pumping, mixing, and agitation. Premixed chemicals, aerosol cans, and household sprayers are good weapons, and the less mixing you have to do at home the better. Choosing a pre-mixed application may limit your choices for some chemicals.

5. Many chemicals are available in dust as well as liquid form. Some are sold as wettable powders—powders you mix with water to form a viscous solution.

   a. Dusts kill insects and eliminate disease quite well. They have to be applied on calm days with no wind, and they usually have to be ingested by bugs or stay on the plant long enough to be effective in disease control. Rain washes them away, and they discolor ornamental plants. They are frequently used in vegetable gardens. Dusts are available in both organic and synthetic formulas.

   b. Wettable powders are not easy to use. They usually have a high viscosity and often clog pressure tank wands. Although they are often inexpensive, they are not nearly as common as they were several years ago. They require frequent agitation to keep the material in suspension, but offer excellent disease control. Some fungicides are available only as wettable powders.

   c. Liquid concentrates are the most popular method of insect and disease control. Easy to use, and packaged for simple mixing, they are combined with water for spray coverage. When used properly, they provide excellent results.

   d. There are several other insecticides and fungicides available to consumers that do not require mixing. Pre-mixed liquids, cans of chemicals propelled by compressed air, pellets that dissolve in water, and household spray bottles of chemicals make treatment simple if you have a single issue.

6. READ THE LABEL COMPLETELY. Mix your chemical carefully. Wear latex gloves, a breathing mask, long-sleeved shirts, and long pants. Do not spill your mixture on the lawn, in the soil of the garden, on the driveway, or on you. Be careful as you pour, mix, and shake.

❧ DR PLANT SAYS: Some concentrates are sold in automatic measuring canisters. Typically, they have a capped spout at the top of the bottle and a side basin for pouring just the right amount into the top cavity. Sometimes you have to tip the bottle slightly to fill the side basin; sometimes you have to squeeze the bottle to spurt the right amount into the basin before it fills the main cavity. This new packaging takes the guesswork out of mixing and is a safe way to measure and mix. DON'T DEFEAT THE FAILSAFE. USE THE BOTTLE CORRECTLY.

7. Pour water into your sprayer or bottle instead of using the garden hose; sudden bursts of water can throw chemicals back into your face. Pour dust into a dusting device at arm's length, turning away from the cloud. Never apply dust straight from the bag, especially with bare hands.

8. Consider using a sticker-spreader. This inert material is mixed with your chemical to help it stick to the target, when applied to the soil and spread through the root system. Often the sticker-spreader contains a coloring agent to help identify it as it is being discharged. You can make your own sticker-spreader by adding a tablespoon of dish detergent to a gallon of mixture.

9. There are two common mistakes made when applying chemicals. One is that "more is better." Completely untrue: using more of a chemical than the recommended dosage is not only wasteful, but also dangerous. Mix the right amount, and apply it at the recommended frequency. Another common mistake is "applying the chemical at half the recommended rate." Don't heed this somewhat popular advice. Read the label and follow the recommended dosages. Using less than the required amount of chemical will only result in disappointment.

10. Mix only what you need, use what you mix, and try to avoid having leftovers.

11. Know your target and mark it plainly. Be aware of the wind, which may carry drift and dust over a large area.

12. What to do with the leftover dust or liquid is a subject not usually addressed in the label instructions. Often, the sole advice provided is "dispose of in approved containers only." If you are using a dust, it is simple to pour the remaining dust back into the original bag, seal it, and store it in the garden tool room. Disposal of liquids is more difficult; discard the contents of the tank or spray bottle into a bucket of sharp sand and dispose of the bucket at your local remediation facility or at a site recommended by the Cooperative Extension Service.

13. Good clean-up is essential. Wash dusters, spray tanks, and all accessories in soapy water, and allow them to dry thoroughly. Be sure to run some clean water through the wand so all chemicals will be cleared.

❦ **DR. PLANT SAYS:** Here are some tips from the pros: That milky color and familiar strong chemical smell that typify most chemical applications are often to remind you of the chemical's potency. Many chemicals are colorless and odorless. You might consider some "dedicated containers." If you use hose-end sprayers to dispense garden chemicals, label them separately, one each for insecticides, fungicides, and herbicides. Finally, the first line of defense should always be an organic chemical. Synthetics are excellent choices, but organic treatments offer some advantages:

   a. They are often more effective than their synthetic counterparts, with better and more rapid results. This is especially true for worm killers.

   b. When applied correctly, they are usually more environmentally friendly than synthetics.

   c. You'll feel safer about using them around your family, pets, and neighbors.

   d. Clean-up is easier.

   e. Disposal is simpler.

   f. Because most organic treatments do not contain the harmful chemicals that synthetics do, there is usually no wait time between application and harvest of vegetables.

❦ **DR. PLANT SAYS:** By law, businesses that sell chemicals must supply information on proper disposal of leftovers, as well as information on the products themselves. You can ask for these information sheets at the counter of the lawn and garden center. They must be available and easily attainable for consumers.

DIAGNOSING AND TRACING PLANT PROBLEMS

WHAT? Diagnosing plant problems and determining their causes is the only way to determine a cure or solution. Otherwise, you'll be guessing at the remedy.

WHO? You should do this yourself.

WHEN? As soon as you notice something wrong with a plant, begin diagnosing the problem.

WHY? In some cases, a problem will be localized to one plant and the solution will be quite simple. In others, serious plant problems will spread through the garden and the solution might be more complicated. Treating a single plant for a minor problem is one thing, but serious diseases and insects can destroy a beautiful landscape in no time. Be observant. As we have said many times, landscape maintenance is a year-round event that involves routine activity. Simple observation on a regular basis will reveal both the healthy and the sick plants in the garden. You can eliminate expensive and time-consuming cures by being observant and treating problems quickly.

WHERE? Treat the problem, of course, but in some cases you may have to prevent it from spreading by treating healthy areas as well. Once you have identified a problem, check to see if it is being replicated in other areas of the landscape, even in neighbors' lawns and gardens. Sometimes their treatment will solve your problems. In many cases, you'll find a cure in the way a friend or neighbor treated a similar problem. Remember the law states that you cannot apply chemicals to a lawn or garden other than your own without a proper permit, so don't offer to spray your neighbors' plants when you treat yours.

HOW? The steps for diagnosing are very basic and should lead to a simple conclusion. If you find the results confusing, it may help to have a second opinion. Once you have determined what you feel is the cause of the problem, verify it with a trip to the Master Gardeners' Plant Clinic in your local area, or take a sample to the Cooperative Extension Service for microscoping and detecting. The more you narrow the possibilities, the more accurate you'll be, and the more time you'll save at the clinic.

You can take a sample to the lawn and garden center or your professional horticulturist for a second opinion. The solution can be determined after several sources agree on the possibilities.

There are only six sources of plant problems. You can have some combinations of these

six, but the direct cause usually comes from one of these alone. In the order of their frequency, they are:
1. Cultural problems
2. Environmental problems
3. Large pests
4. Diseases
5. Insects
6. None of the above

   1. *Cultural problems* are related to the way you cultivate and maintain the garden and lawn, and arise from either too much care or lack of care. Some typical problems are:
* **Too much water.** This problem manifests itself in many ways: sunken areas in lawn grasses, moldy areas, slimy sections of lawn or turf, plants that wilt frequently from "drowning," an oily sheen on foliage from iron bacteria, heavy, excessive growth, or too many weeds in the garden.
* **Not enough water.** Wilted or dead plants, brown grass, improper blooming in the spring, poor bulb performance in the spring and summer, poor vegetable yield, slow terminal growth, small leaves, and general plant lethargy are all indications of a lack of water.
* **Improper pH balancing.** Too much lime on the lawn results in pale lawn grass. Acid soil results in stunted•plants, leaves that are small, stunted or pale, plants that are unable to absorb some nutrients, insignificant flowers, poor yield, and plants or grass that look "tired" and weak.
* **Over-use of fertilizers.** Excessive use of fertilizer can result in too much top growth too quickly, plants that fade quickly in the heat of the summer from lack of root development, increased numbers of insects crowding nitrogen-rich plants, poor flowers from "lazy" plants that are overfed, bulbs with no flowers, or too much lawn grass.
* **Improper mowing.** Brown or dead areas can be caused by scalping. Repetition of the same mowing patterns creates depressions and poor performance. Other mistakes are cutting the lawn too often or too short.
* **Improper pruning.** Poor flowering, erratic terminal growth, the need for continued and repeated pruning, large swollen areas of trunks and branches, distorted plant shapes, failure of plants to regenerate growth in some specific places following pruning, diseases and insects that invade open wounds, torn bark and split limbs can all result from improper pruning.
* **Improper drainage.** Plants subjected to improper drainage will exhibit the same symptoms as plants that receive too much water. Eventually, they will wilt and die.
* **Poor plant selection.** You will encounter problems if you choose difficult plants to raise, plants that are known to be fickle or not suited for the area, plants with odd foliage shapes

and colors, untried and untested varieties, unknown grafts, plants with weedy appearances and odd growth habits, or plants from foreign countries that should not be grown in your area.

• **Lack of knowledge about plant performance.** Common mistakes are: treating annuals as perennials and having them fail in their second season, disregarding specific requirements for protection, or ignoring or not knowing a plant's susceptibility to disease and insect invasion.

• **Misuse of herbicides and chemicals.** Care must be taken to prevent weed killers from drifting onto foliage or into your neighbor's garden. Improper use of chemicals or chemical drift from neighbors' gardens may cause plants to die outright or have their foliage desiccated. Labels should be read carefully and directions followed precisely.

• **Improper fertilizing.** Flower buds that fail to open, flowers that fall off before blooming, poor plant performance, poor color, lack of growth, or general lethargy can all result from improper fertilizing.

• **Poor nursery stock.** Some container-grown stock may be rootbound, have faulty root systems, be overdeveloped for the pot size, or have experienced faulty growing techniques that have created a sub-standard plant from the outset.

Changing the way you cultivate the garden solves cultural problems. Solutions take time, and are not always easy. The best way to avoid cultural problems is to know the requirements of the plants you are raising, and follow a basic plan of good health. It is always better to approach the culture of your lawn and garden from a positive position of maintaining good culture and good health rather than from a standpoint of problem-solving and crisis management.

2. *Environmental problems* are caused by events in nature that are usually beyond your control. The effects of natural calamities can sometimes be lessened, but when environmental events cause problems, the cures are often time-consuming and laborious.

• **Freeze damage.** Sudden freezes kill plants and flowers, while slow, steady drops in temperature will create copper-colored foliage. Ground freezing kills root systems, which causes the plant to wilt and die. Frost gives a burned appearance to lawns and gardens. Flowers and plants may fail to bloom the following season if freeze damage is severe.

• **Severe heat.** Obvious burning effects include sunburned foliage and flowers. Heat may also cause sunken spots appear on leaves and flowers, plants that wilt and fail to make fruits, and flowers that fail to open. In general, the garden appears weak and lethargic.

• **Excessive humidity.** Wilted plants, molds and mildews, increased insect activity, weak plants, and limp and pale foliage are all indications of high humidity.

• **Too much sudden rainfall.** A heavy downpour can drown plants, wash seeds from beds, leach fertilizers, uproot plants, cause bulbs to rot, cause flooding, create weed invasions, create fire ant mounds in new places, and cause depressions in the lawn.

• **Hail.** Broken limbs and destroyed foliage and flowers are all obvious results of damaging hail.

• **Lightning.** Large trees and surrounding landscape plants can be killed by lightning, although sometimes death is slow and takes place months after the initial strike. Tree scarring can result, and lightning wounds attract borers and insects.

• **Utility line breaks.** Sewer line breaks create biohazards. Septic tank overflows create too much growth or kill sections of the lawn or garden, in addition to creating foul smells. Underground electric line breaks can destroy plants' root systems, and utility line crews doing maintenance work can create soil compaction or other damage. Water softener discharge lines inject water into the ground, creating wilted plants and killing color gardens.

• **Chemical spills.** Such spills can kill plants outright, or may create stunted plants that fail to recover quickly. Gasoline spills discolor and kill plants.

Fertilizer spills give a burned appearance to sections of the lawn and garden. Household cleaners, paint, and paint thinners can kill plants or sections of them.

• **Snow and ice.** In addition to broken branches, snow and ice have obvious effects on the garden. Although snow insulates foliage and turf from severe freezing, it adds weight to plants, and hedges that have been pruned as "flat tops" can be damaged by the extra weight to the extent that the shape is permanently altered. Ice and snow are seldom seen along the coast, though freak storms have hit the area. Ice damage often comes from irrigation systems that are left running during freezing weather.

• **Graft failure.** Expensive plant grafts, grafted roses, and hybrid fruit trees that fail often do so because of the failure of the graft itself. If the graft fails, the top of the plant dies and the understock continues to grow. This results in water sprouts and shoots growing from a plant that is inferior to the one purchased.

• **Nutrient deficiencies.** These deficiencies can create oddly shaped flowers, poor appearance, lethargic plants, irregular growth habits, copper-colored leaves, spotted or mottled foliage, stunted plants, weak plants that break easily, yellowing, general die-back, poor lawn grass performance, sickly appearances, and plants and gardens that die in extreme weather conditions or fail to support good growth. (Nutrient deficiencies create overall poor performance, not isolated instances where one part of the plant fails.)

• **Improper pollination or failure to pollinate.** Flowers fail to open; flowers are lacking or oddly shaped; flowers fail to make fruits or produce stunted fruits; vegetables have strange shapes and sizes.

If you suspect that the environment has caused the problem with which you are dealing, don't hesitate to mention this to your plant professional as you diagnose the problem. Using a pesticide to correct an environmental problem may only add to the problem.

3. *Large pests* occur in most lawns and gardens, and they cannot be avoided. Fortunately, they are easy to control—or at least their damage is easily repaired.
- **You.** You are the pest that creates most problems in the landscape, so be careful how you cultivate the lawn and garden.
- **Weeds.** They harbor insects that invade the garden, extract vital nutrients and water, crowd plants in the color garden, diminish flowering and fruiting, create poor appearances, shadow more delicate plants, hide seedlings, and overrun mulched beds.
- **Large animals.** Deer eat plants from all sides; dogs and cats "mark" territories with feces and urine, creating burned sections of the lawn and garden; squirrels uproot bulbs and some garden plants, and disturb the garden with their seed-burying; rabbits eat plant tops; and raccoons disturb the garden with their foraging.
- **Small animals.** Moles and voles tunnel through the soft lawn just under the surface. Though moles do not eat plants, they can cause you to trip and stumble in their runways, and field rats use the same tunnels. Voles eat roots and below-ground plant parts.
- **Lawn and garden equipment.** Lawn tractors can damage the lawn; line-trimmers girdle some plants, causing them to wilt and die; shrubs can be destroyed by lawn mowers, seedlings can be destroyed by leaf blowers; and plants can be wounded by equipment bumps and strikes. Bicycles and other recreation toys often cause plant disorders.

4. *Plant diseases* are often considered the main culprits in gardens that perform poorly, though they are rarely as damaging as some may think. Healthy plants can be very resistant to disease, and those plants that seem to get sick frequently should be avoided in your garden plan. Native plants are usually tolerant of most growing conditions, and are often disease-free. If you concentrate on building a healthy landscape featuring native and adapted plants, you'll have few disease problems.

Though nematodes are not diseases, they appear in this listing because their effects often resemble disease symptoms. The only sure way to diagnose root-killing nematodes is to dig the plant. These nematodes can be controlled with several types of organic nematicides. Foliar nematodes, however, cannot be controlled. If you suspect nematodes in your vegetable garden, you can take a sample of the soil from around the roots of the affected plants to the Cooperative Extension Service for testing. Though results may be slow in coming, a good diagnosis is available.
- **Bacterial diseases.** These diseases cause plants to wilt or lose foliage, and sections of the plant may die quickly from no apparent cause. Tree trunks have open lesions that ooze foul-smelling discharge; broken stems have black centers with rotten sections; plants discharge

sap; leaves and plant tissue display large sunken depressions. Diagnosis is incomplete without examining stem sections and cross-sections of tissue. (Bacterial diseases usually have no cure.)

• **Viral diseases.** Some obvious characteristics are stippled foliage, leaf color variegation, yellowing of leaves and leaf margins, distorted flowers and fruits, dramatic color changes in plant parts, or twisted growth. Whole sections of the plant may die slowly or plant parts may fail. Stunted growth may occur in part or all of the plant. Flowers may fail to open or flowers may bloom poorly. Viral diseases have no cure.

• **Fungal diseases.** These most common plant diseases are difficult to diagnose correctly because there are so many fungi that are pathogenic. If you suspect nematodes, bacterial disorders, or viral infections, make sure you have the correct diagnosis before you begin treatment. Fungal diseases are easy to control with commercial fungicides if they are applied to unaffected parts of the plant, or poured through the soil to correct soil-borne fungal diseases. Symptoms of fungal disease include: lower stem parts that show black circles and cause wilting of the upper parts; stems with sunken, black sections; fruits with open lesions with watery discharge; leaves with abnormal growths (galls and foliage edema); molds and mildews on leaves and flowers, soot and powdery mildew on foliage and flowers; and oily, slick patches on lawn grasses. Root-rotting fungal diseases cause upper parts of plants to turn yellow and wilt or leaves to have target-like spots and extreme color variegation. Fungal blights "singe" leaf margins and shred the edges of foliage, or cause new growth to suddenly curls and die. Leaves and flowers will develop purple spots; flowers displaying greasy patches will suddenly wilt and fall to the ground. Sunken, wet areas will appear in fruits and foliage, and leaves and stems will become discolored, dry and brittle.

Treating diseases can be a chore that requires persistence and the correct choice of weapons. Be patient and allow all the time needed to show results.

5. *Insects* are often unfairly blamed for many garden problems. Many insects are beneficial and aid in controlling other insects and diseases. Because you can often see the pest, diagnosing insect problems is somewhat easier than diagnosing other plant problems. There are thousands of insects in the garden; if you suspect one is causing a problem, take a sample to the Master Gardeners Clinic or the Extension Service for identification. The right insecticide depends on the target insect.

• **Worms.** They eat sections of leaves, leaf margins, whole leaves, and some plant parts. Worms and caterpillars are often found on the undersides of the leaves, or along the branches and stems of plants during the heat of the day or daylight hours. Worms are often active at night as well. Maggots (also known as midges) are often microscopic and can't be seen as they eat leaf margins. Caterpillars bore through stems, into fruit, into flower parts. They cause plant parts to wilt, whole plants to wilt, or seedlings to topple.

• **Snails and slugs.** These creatures feed at night on plant parts, leaves, and flowers by eating the leaf margins, sections of flowers, and tender stems. The can destroy whole sections of color gardens in a few short days.

• **Beetles.** They eat leaf margins, create shot-hole appearances in leaves, destroy flowers, bore inside young flower buds, eat whole plant parts, and leave telltale signs of their progress.

• **Soft-bodied insects.** These insects are the most common plant insect pests and are easily identified by their webs and obvious appearances. Spider mites are hard to see, but often have webs. Aphids are tiny insects that live and thrive in massive colonies. Woolly aphids have a sticky, cottony residue.

White flies scatter when disturbed, creating clouds of insects. Soft-bodied insects suck the sap from plant parts, creating yellow foliage and weak plant parts, poor flowering, and wilting. They are often "vectors" of diseases, spreading fungal disorders as they feed.

• **Scales.** These soft-bodied insects live in crusty shells that form on stems, foliage, and plant parts. The cause yellow foliage, sooty molds, leaf loss, and general plant failure.

• **Odd insects.** This group includes leaf miners that tunnel between layers of foliage leaving yellow patterns of lines in leaves, mole crickets that destroy grass roots and grass foliage, huge caterpillars like the tomato hornworm that devour whole leaves, and tiny wire-worms that eat stems and plant parts.

Problem insects are easy to diagnose; you either see them directly causing the problem, or you see the signs of their damage. The damage they cause by eating plant parts is obvious. Less noticeable is their discharge on affected plant parts. This discharge is often called "frass," and attracts other insects as well as fungal diseases. Because some feed at night, you may have to use a flashlight to see them at work, but taking a sample of what's bugging you can lead to a quick and simple solution. Insecticides are quite common and easy to use. Just make sure that killing these pests is to your advantage.

6. *"None of the above"* is a catch-all section for the unexplained. Nature is not exact. Diagnosing plant problems is sometimes fruitless and, as with anything in the natural kingdom, there are unusual phenomena. Not every problem has a solution; not every situation has an explanation. Responsible horticulturists recognize the ever-changing nature of the environment and the complex world of botany. It would be foolish to assume that everything can be explained. Sometimes it is within the nature of the plant itself to perform at some levels. Many plants don't live up to expectations, and all the sprays, powders, and treatments in the world won't change them. Be prepared for the unexplainable. In the amazing world of plant biology, anything can happen.

VERY BASIC LANDSCAPE DESIGN

WHAT? Designing a landscape layout or simple garden design.

WHO? You can make a basic landscape plan with some simple considerations.

WHEN? Complete this project before you actually do any landscaping work in your new garden.

WHY? Simply put, your chances of creating the ideal lawn and garden for your place will be much improved if you have a good plan before you start. This plan doesn't need to be complicated; in fact, it doesn't even need to be drawn to scale. It just needs to be thought out in advance with some goal or idea of what you expect your landscape to accomplish.

WHERE? Any renovation project, new landscape design, or new garden should be planned.

HOW? Approach your new garden as if it were a room in a house. It will have the same basic requirements that any room would have, especially a room that is used often.

1. The ceiling should be the sky, of course, but you can also plan on some canopy. What types of trees would you like above the garden? Spring-flowering trees? Deciduous trees? Do you want a green canopy all year? Consider fall color. What colors of fall foliage would you like to see? The winter "ceiling" can be very impressive, with trees bearing a stark winter skyline with many branches, or trees that have few branches but a large spreading crown. Any ceiling has lights, so you'll want to plan on allowing enough sunlight through the canopy to support turf and flowering plants below.

2. The "walls" of the room are the barriers of shrubbery you'll install along its perimeters. How high and wide should they be? Do you want consistency, or would you prefer having a mixture of plants, textures, and foliage? Would you like flowering plants or evergreen shrubs? Walls have windows, of course, and you might want to plan your garden to have some exposure through the walls to see beyond your property line. Capitalize on the available views so that windows in your room afford optimum views. Solid walls obstruct some sights. On the other hand, you may want to hide some things from view. Tall hedges and screens can be walls that hide neighbors' yards from sight, making yours more private and secure.
    Be sure to leave enough space in the walls for entrances and exits. Corners may be the

perfect places for large trees that anchor the room and connect the ceiling with the floor.

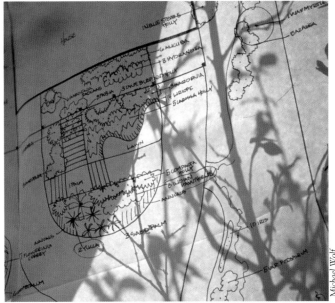

Michael Wolf

3. Speaking of the floor, you should decide right away which covering you want. Is lawn your choice? Remember that the more turf you have, the higher your maintenance will be. It's like having carpet in the house; you'll have to keep it clean. Would another floor covering be a better choice? How about hardscaping? Would a floor of natural material, combined with flagstones, pavers, or mulch, be better than a lawn? And don't forget the traffic pattern between entrances and exits; a well-worn path might be acceptable, or you might consider a walkway of different construction.

4. No room is complete without furniture and appointments, so you'll want to make space for some flowerbeds and featured landscaped sections of the area. Mixed beds are popular, and feature combinations of plants and flowering shrubbery. They can be placed anywhere as long as the sunlight is strong enough to support good growth. Massed plantings, such as annual color gardens that feature one-of-a-kind flowering plants, are popular features in modern landscapes. Areas that are left as nature designed them are maintenance-free sections of the landscape, and specimen plantings that feature single ornamentals that are the best examples of what that particular plant should be. Specimen plants should be featured close to doors and windows of the actual house so that you can see them from many angles, watching them as they change seasons.

5. Accessories are often the landscape items that make a "room" in the garden an extension of your lifestyle and a reflection of your individuality. Wind chimes and bird feeders, garden statuaries and benches are examples of accessories that give your landscape a distinctive character. Like pictures on the walls, lamps, and art objects, landscape accessories define your creativity. Sundials, birdbaths, birdhouses, and swings are items that make your landscape a part of your home, not just the object of weekly maintenance.

In designing your landscape as you would any room in the house, you create a unique atmosphere in your total home site that allows you to move from one room to another, inside or outdoors, each area connected by your lifestyle.

❦ **DR. PLANT SAYS:** Don't rely totally on professionals to design your landscape. Take an active part in planning. Your landscape will be more enjoyable for you and your family if it reflects your lifestyle.

Freda Wilkins

HOW TO DETERMINE SUNLIGHT EXPOSURE

WHAT? Plants perform best when they have the right exposure to sunlight. The proper exposure varies greatly from one plant to the next. Sunlight triggers blooming, contributes to overall health, helps to control disease, builds healthy foliage, and stimulates growth. Plants that have less than the amount of required sunlight never live up to expectations, and those that get too much can suffer "sunburn" as well as severe wilting that will gradually weaken or even kill the plant.

Most plants sold in nurseries have tell-tags that describe ideal sunlight requirements. Following these recommendations will not guarantee success, but your chances of success will be improved if your plant has the best exposure from the start. Moving plants at a later date to change exposure is risky.

WHO? You can do this yourself, or make sure your landscaper or gardener does it before plants are installed in the garden.

WHEN? Determine the best location for your new plant, based on exposure, before you put it into the garden.

WHY? You should expect ideal performance from any plant, not marginal success. Forcing plants to perform in less-than-ideal locations usually results in disappointment.

WHERE? Every location in your landscape probably has some sunlight exposure, and there are some simple ways to determine what that exposure is. By comparing the minimum and maximum amount of sunlight in a specific place to the amount recommended on the plant information tag, you can determine the best place for your plant.

HOW? There are four exposures used by most plant specialists to illustrate the best locations for a plant:

1. **Full Sun** is unfiltered, uninterrupted sunlight between 10:00 a.m. and 4:00 p.m. If you hold your hand over a plant in full exposure, you should get a definite shadow during these hours. Plants that are rated for full sun need a great deal of sunshine for optimum growth and development, but along the coast, that sunlight can be very hot. Morning sun warms plants faster than afternoon sun, but it is also a "cooler" light. Direct afternoon sunlight is intense, and can create wilting and even sunburn.

2. **Partial Sun** is almost the same amount of light as full sun, but the light is dappled or filtered for two of the hours. Five or six hours of direct sunlight is required for plants listed for "partial sun," but that light can be filtered, as through a high canopy of overhanging trees. Pine trees often provide ideal filtering of sunlight. Classic Southern plants rated for full sun often perform better in partial sun because the heat is not as intense.

3. **Partial shade** is often called "indirect light". Though the term is often confused with "partial sun," it is actually quite different. The five or six hours of sunlight required for optimum growth in full sun or partial sun is reduced by an hour, so four hours of sunlight are required. The intensity can be dappled or filtered for the entire amount of time, and the remainder of the daylight sunshine should be filtered as well. Tall trees, shade trees and natural screens often provide the filters for bright coastal sun.

4. **Full Shade** is the coolest exposure and offers the least amount of sunlight. Plants grown in full shade receive little, if any direct sunlight and are usually grown under dense canopy or next to buildings that offer constant shade from the sun. There are not many plants recommended for full shade exposure.

The sun rises in the east. As it progresses in the course of the day, it passes through southern exposure, is directly overhead at noon, and sets in the west.
1. Plants with eastern and southeastern exposures generally meet the full sun requirement by getting enough sunlight in the morning hours up until early afternoon.
2. Plants that have only southeastern exposure probably meet the requirements for partial sun. They may not get the direct heat of the midday sun.
3. Plants with western exposure often get five hours of sunlight from noon until five o'clock. They also get the brunt of the heat because of the hot midday sun.
4. Plants with northern exposure get little direct sunlight and often spend the day in shade.

❦ **DR. PLANT SAYS:** Orientation to the sun is not always the best way to determine how much sunlight a location will get. You need to test the site, especially because buildings shade garden spots. Testing is easy; simply observe the location for a day, and measure the amount of sunlight falling on the spot. Don't be surprised if a building, tall trees, or even parked cars obscure sunlight, causing the location to change exposures.

THE MOST COMMON MISTAKES IN GARDENING

WHAT? These are simple mistakes, yet they contribute to poor landscape performance and can often lead to plant failure. In some cases, these mistakes lead homeowners to be so dissatisfied with their landscapes that whole gardens are eradicated and re-established.

WHO? These common mistakes can cause problems for you or the people who maintain your garden.

WHEN? These mistakes usually occur at the time that plants are placed in the landscape, but if the garden is not maintained, mistakes can create problems at any stage of the process.

WHY? You might assume that lack of knowledge is the main cause, but neglect is a major mistake in lawn and garden maintenance.

WHERE? Right in your own lawn and garden, of course. As you can see from the list, many mistakes occur before any actual planting takes place.

HOW? Listed in the order of their frequency, the most common landscaping mistakes leading to plant problems are:

1. Planting too deeply
2. Insufficient water
3. Neglect
4. Too much water
5. Wrong location, wrong exposure -
   a. Plants too close together
   b. Plants too close to the foundation or house
   c. Plants too sparse or too far apart for best show
6. Damage from any source
7. Poor plant selection
8. Improper fertilization—too much or too little
9. Incorrect pruning
10. Incorrect pH

HOW TO INSTALL SOD

WHAT? Replacing a lawn or establishing a lawn from sod is the quickest way to generate turf. Seeding is a popular method, but installing rolled sod is the most popular way of creating a lawn.

WHO? Installing sod is a tedious task, but you can do it by following these simple instructions. If you hire someone for the job, be sure to supervise your investment.

WHEN? Though installing sod can be done at any time, it is best to do this job in early spring when active grass is readily available. Purchasing and installing dormant, brown sod is inadvisable because you can't see the health and vitality of the grass. A lawn from sod installed in early spring generates a quality turf by summer's end, and provides a finished turf in a short time during the growing season.

WHY? In today's world, there is little time to care for a seeded lawn. It takes a lot of care and time to raise a lawn from seed. You'll have faster results from sod, and fewer cultural requirements.

WHERE? Once you have established the type of turf you want, and the sunlight requirements are met, you can sod any section of your landscape, provided the soil is suitable for raising lawn grass.

HOW? Follow these basic instructions:

1. Remove the existing lawn with a sod cutter. (Though you can use herbicides to kill grass and weeds, you will always have a better base for new sod if you remove the existing growth completely with a sod cutter, available from a rental company).

2. Modify the soil with conditioners, or starter fertilizers if needed, then rake and level the area. Using a roller half-filled with water, smooth the new bed, making sure that the level of the soil is an inch below patios, driveways, and walkways to accommodate the thickness of the sod.

3. Measure the square footage that you are covering, and purchase all the sod you will need for the entire project. Allow ample time to complete the job from start to finish.

4. Water the bare soil of the new bed.

5. Start laying the sod at the longest straight-away, from boundary to boundary. Install it as you would lay brick—staggering the sections. No seams! Make sure each section fits tightly against the previous one without overlapping edges. New sod must come into excellent contact with the soil beneath it. If the ground is wet or soft, use a piece of plywood on which to kneel.

6. Use a sharp butcher knife or sod knife to cut sections to fit, working around corners and into angles. If you are covering a slope, start at the bottom and work to the top, securing the new sod with heavy "hairpins" or stakes.

7. As soon as you have a small section complete, begin watering—don't wait until the end of the project. Never let new sod dry out.

8. Roll the entire area with a roller as soon as the job is complete. Water every day until the new grass is spongy underfoot, morning and afternoon, if necessary. Make sure the new sod stays moist. Do this for ten days, then check to see if new roots are visible by lifting a corner of the sod. Once good rooting has taken place, you can reduce soaking the lawn to a few days each week. As soon as you have established your lawn, and have cut it once, water at the recommended rate for your type of turf.

❧ **DR. PLANT SAYS:** Many Cooperative Extension Services offer lawn grass test sites where different types of turf are displayed. Visiting one of these displays can help determine which turf suits your interests. At the same time, you can also gain some specific information about installing turf.

COLD TOLERANCE IN PLANTS AND HOW TO PROTECT PLANTS FROM FREEZE DAMAGE

WHAT? Most of the plants in your landscape will not need much protection from severe winter weather. In the event of a severe freeze warning, or if you are concerned about the ability of your sensitive plants to survive a cold snap, there are some things you can do to lessen the damage. Bear in mind that prolonged freezing weather will ultimately damage many coastal plants.

WHO? You can protect your sensitive plants from winter freeze damage, or you can hire someone to do it for you.

WHEN? Freezes and severe cold weather come without much warning; all you may have is a day or two to get ready. The average temperature in the coldest month of the year along the coast is fifty-four degrees, and the lowest mean temperature is thirty-three, so you certainly can't keep plants bundled up for the entire winter. If you wrap a plant to prevent freezing one day, you may have to remove the wrap the next. Keep an eye on the weather. If you find that temperatures are going to be excessively cold for longer than a day or two, proceed with some protection, but be prepared to remove the cover quickly.

WHY? It would be a shame to lose a valuable plant just because the weather became extreme for a brief period. It has happened to nearly every gardener, but there may be some simple things you can do to avoid serious injury. If you do nothing at all in the event of a freeze, you may be quite safe, but why run the risk?

WHERE? Any place in the garden that is threatened can be protected, and any plant can be secured.

HOW? Following are some helpful facts about freezing and some plants' abilities to resist cold weather damage:

1. Water freezes at thirty-two degrees, but the water inside a plant's vascular system may not drop that low even though the outside temperature is thirty-two or colder.

2. The sap inside a plant has components other than water which often lower its freezing temperature.

3. Frost is frozen dew. It can do as much damage to foliage as freezing temperatures, but rarely does damage to stems and branches.

4. Plants that face direct northern winds without protection often suffer freeze damage even earlier than do plants with more protection from buildings, fences, or other structures.

5. Snow often protects plants from severe freeze damage because it insulates plants from freezing winds. Once the plant is "sealed" by a layer of snow, it usually gets no colder than the snow around it.

6. The speed with which the temperature drops to below freezing is important in calculating potential damage. If the temperature drops slowly and stays below freezing for an extended amount of time, the damage from freezing will be greater. If the temperature drops rapidly and then rises quickly, potential damage will be far less severe.

Freda Wilkins

7. Plants that face southeast often stand a greater chance of damage during days of prolonged freezing temperatures. As the sun heats the bark during the day, fluids naturally rise in the stem tissue. Later in the evening, the liquid in the stem freezes as the intensity of the sunlight decreases and temperatures drop.

8. Severe freeze damage happens when bark splits and cells burst. There is little a plant can do to repair this type of damage. Once the bark or interior cell structure is frozen enough to cause expansion and retraction of the tissue itself, the result is usually damage beyond repair. You'll have to prune away this type of frozen wood.

9. The worst possible freeze damage takes place when the root systems of plants freeze. Ground freezing kills plants quickly.

10. Some plants are tougher than others. Not all plants suffer damage at 32 degrees, and some will fail completely if the temperature drops to 32 degrees for just a few minutes.

Here are some ways you can protect your valuable plants from freezing weather:

1. Protect the root system of all your landscape plants throughout the winter with dry garden mulch.

2. Keep your plants well watered through the winter season so they stay healthy.

3. Avoid excessive pruning during the winter months.

4. In the event of a freeze warning, you can wrap a plant with any material except plastic sheeting. Plastic sheets generate a great deal of heat in sun exposure and can cause severe wilting and actual heat damage even on the coldest winter day. Old blankets, newsprint, bed sheets, and even clothing can be used to protect plants from below-freezing temperatures. Whatever material you decide to use, secure it so the wrap is tight and won't blow away in windy weather.

5. A conservative method of freeze protection is a simple wire cage, such as a tomato cage, placed around the plant and filled with dry leaves or garden refuse. Rolled and crumbled newsprint are also good fillers.

6. Don't add additional weight to the branches of plants when you wrap them.

7. Remember that along the coast, rainy weather usually brings southerly airflow that warms the atmosphere. It can be freezing one night with rain on the way, but temperatures can rise rapidly as the rain approaches.

8. Air circulation and sunshine are essential to good garden health. Get the wraps off the plants as soon as possible.

9. Don't "ice over" plants with your lawn sprinklers and irrigation system in the event of freezing weather. Ice damages limbs and branches far more than it protects them from cold temperatures.

HOW TO USE A HOSE-END SPRAYER

WHAT? Hose-end sprayers are designed to dispense liquid chemical applications with the assistance of a garden hose. Attached to the end of the hose, the canister holds the proper amount of pre-measured chemicals. As water passes over or through the canister, the correct amount of chemical is metered into the water and applied to the target. The process is simple and convenient.

WHO? You can easily use this convenient lawn and garden tool with little trouble if you understand how it works and how to mix the chemicals you plan to dispense.

WHEN? There are many ways to dispense chemicals in the lawn and garden. Compressed-air sprayers (pressure sprayers) are the most familiar, but they require mixing chemicals with water and pumping air into the tank to propel the mixture. Hose-end sprayers are simpler to operate, and should be used whenever possible. There are times, however, when a compressed-air sprayer might be a better tool: reaching high limbs, spraying delicate plants, hitting specific targets in tight surroundings are a few of these instances. Whenever a choice is available, however, use a hose-end sprayer.

WHY? A quality-made hose-end sprayer is easy to use and minimizes confusion when mixing chemicals. One-hand operation is simple and less work than carrying a heavy compressed-air sprayer. You'll avoid mixing chemicals in a tank, and your standard garden hose will do most of the work for you.

WHERE? Use a hose-end sprayer for most chemical applications that require broad-spectrum applications. They are perfect for applying fertilizers or herbicides to lawn grasses, water-soluble fertilizers to annual color gardens and vegetable gardens, and soapy-water solutions to many plants. There are other uses for these sprayers; you can wash your car with them, or use them to help clean lawn furniture and apply detergents to decks and patios.

HOW? Hose-end sprayers work on a simple principle. The lid attachment to the canister contains a connection for the hose end and a tube that extends into the canister. Water passing over the tube and canister creates a vacuum that absorbs the contents of the canister and mixes it with the water as it leaves the canister lid. In better hose-end sprayers, a dial attached to the lid regulates the amount of chemical absorbed. When the task or project is complete, the remaining chemical can be poured back into its original container.

These suggestions should be helpful in using a hose-end sprayer:

1. **Purchase the best equipment possible.** I recommend the Gilmour model 499. There are many types and styles of hose-end sprayers, but this particular model offers a number of

advantages for simple use by homeowners. It has a dial that indicates the rate of application per thousand square feet and the correct mixture rate. Mixing takes place in the head of the canister, not in the canister itself, so there is no pre-mixing of chemicals with water. Simply pour the correct amount of chemical into the canister, secure the lid, and turn on the water.

Some hose-end sprayers require mixing water with chemicals in the canister before applying. Avoid these types of sprayers—the instructions for mixing and proper dispensing can be confusing.

While some hose-end sprayers specify amounts of chemicals to be applied in ounces per gallon, others specify teaspoons or tablespoons per gallon. It is always better to use a hose-end sprayer that contains an easy-to-read conversion chart. In the case of the Gilmour model, the chart is directly linked to the dial, so measuring chemicals and square footage is easy to understand. Simply pour the amount of chemical into the canister, set the dial to the correct square footage, and apply the material.

2. **Hose-end sprayers work best with herbicides and water-soluble fertilizers.** For all other chemical applications, it is best to use a different tool—a household sprayer or pressure sprayer, for example.

3. **Use dedicated sprayers.** Even though it is expensive to purchase several hose-end sprayers, you should have one for fertilizers and one for herbicides, each labeled for its specific task.

4. **Make sure your hose and connections are secure.** No leaks!

5. **Wettable powders don't work well with hose-end sprayers.** Use liquid chemicals or water-soluble fertilizers only.

6. **Before you begin the project, measure a typical amount of territory** so you'll be familiar with the area to be sprayed and the amount of chemical that is going to be applied over the area according to the dial. For example, if the area you are spraying is five hundred square feet, pace five hundred square feet before you start so you'll know how large the treatment area is.

7. **Rather than mixing the largest amount of chemical for the largest amount of area, begin your project by applying the smallest amount of chemical to the smallest amount of area.** You can increase the dosage and square footage later, as you become comfortable with the way the hose-end sprayer is working. In other words, if you have a choice of one tablespoon

for five hundred square feet, or three tablespoons for fifteen hundred square feet, choose the smaller amount for the first application and set the dial accordingly. As you become familiar with the tool and application, you can increase the rate.

8. **Safety First!** Remember to follow label instructions to the letter, and wear protective clothing. Wear a pair of latex gloves in case of leaks, and be sure to have proper eyewear. Drifting spray is always a concern when using herbicides, so be aware of the surrounding landscape.

9. **Never modify the tool.** Don't try to change the spray pressure by adding an adjustable nozzle to the spray head. Don't alter the way the canister feeds. Be sure to leave safety features in place.

Michael Wolf